❖ Joliet Girl ❖

❖ JOLIET GIRL ❖

FRANCINE MARIE TOLF

NORTH STAR PRESS OF ST. CLOUD, INC.
St. Cloud, Minnesota

Credits

These essays appeared in the following publications:

"Becoming a Writer: Nine," "Becoming a Writer: Twelve," *Dust & Fire*
"My Dad, Finally," *Green Hills Literary Lantern*
"The Summer Before Eighth Grade," *Toasted Cheese*
"Halcyon Days," *Under the Sun*

ISBN-10: 9-87839-371-4
ISBN-13: 978-0-87839-371-8

First Edition: June 2010

Printed in the United States of America

Published by
North Star Press of St. Cloud, Inc.
P.O. Box 451
St. Cloud, Minnesota 56302

northstarpress.com

Contents

TO THE READER

Addressing you like this may seem a little old-fashioned, but I wanted to tell you why I wrote this book. I had a home once. I had a neighborhood. I was part of a large, loving family. I never doubted, when I was growing up, that I would always be close with my five older sisters. If someone had told me there would come a day when I was on easy speaking terms with only two, I would not have believed it.

The family closeness I took for granted as a child fascinates me. It forms the bedrock of who I am as a human being and as a writer. Yet the house I remember as filled with light was hardly the site of a perfect childhood, and the relationships that underlay my first twelve years contained inevitabilities that sometimes played out in painful ways.

Maybe that's why I feel compelled to write about my childhood. I thought the answer was simpler: what was once is no more. I saw this book as my way of preserving a small, personal piece of the past. This alone is certainly a powerful incentive. The family I was part of, the town I once knew, and the home I grew up in, more familiar and more deeply loved than any of the homes that followed, exist now only in memory. Hardly surprising that I would want to write about them.

It's not that I'm not grateful for the life I have today. I have a good man who loves me, some dear friends, two cats I adore—and my writing. But once I belonged to something bigger than myself, and that's no longer true. I don't identify with a particular community or ethnicity or religion. If I walk into a Catholic church nowadays, it's like revisiting a country after many years and finding that it is utterly foreign. I like Minneapolis, the city where Marc and I live, but I have no history here. I'm not really part of any writing community, either. Writing is a solitary business.

Memoirist Patricia Hampl calls memory "the final refuge of the dispossessed." Maybe someone who has never been forced by violence or by natural disaster to uproot has no right to claim these words, but sometimes I feel dispossessed. I think there are a lot of such dispossessed Americans today: women and men whose ties with their nuclear families and the faiths they grew up with and the home towns they knew intimately have snapped. People who have relocated half a dozen times, people carrying their own versions of what was once and is gone.

I didn't know it, but I started writing *Joliet Girl* in the spring of 2004, when I wrote an essay about my mother. She had died six years earlier at the age of seventy-nine. "Old age isn't for the faint of heart," my mother observed to me once, with grim humor. The last two years of her life proved the truth of those words. They included caring for my father, her beloved Arthur, at home, even though he no longer knew who she was. Not long after his death, Mom lost her dearest sister, Marjorie. Less than a year later, in July of 1997, she received a call from St. Francis Hospital in Evanston informing her that Gale Tolf, her forty-three-year-old daughter, had been hit by a car and was in intensive care.

My mother admitted herself to the hospital that August. She was so tired, she said. She never returned home. She died in September. Decades before, she used to sing about September, her favorite month, as she did laundry in the basement or chopped carrots for stew at the kitchen table: "Try to remember the days of September and follow, follow, follow . . ." How sweet and sad that melody sounded to me when I was a child! I loved the lull and roll of the rhymes, the magical invitation to *follow, follow, follow.* I understood instinctively that whatever mysterious place my mother was singing about could never be entered again by those people in the song, no matter how badly they wanted to return to it.

My mother's death did not consume me with grief as I thought it would. I knew how ill she was; days before she died, a doctor told me that all of her major organs were breaking down. I was thankful she was no longer suffering. Somehow our relationship felt like a deep stream that continued to flow. It was what happened between me and my sisters that devastated.

I used to think loss of closeness among siblings was the exception rather than the rule. Now I'm not so sure. Political and religious views, economics, having or not having children of one's own, are all potential dividers as sisters and brothers grow older. So are issues that festered in childhood and don't come to a head until later: the inevitabilities that play out in painful ways.

I address those inevitabilities in this book. You'll learn exactly how a once close set of sisters became distanced from one another. But I want first to linger a bit on my early years. They're my wellspring. Let me tell you about them.

FAMILY TREE

My Father's Parents
Alvar Tolf
Olga Gustaphson

My Mother's Parents
Michael Kelly
Florence Potch

Their Children
Rueben
Albert
Arthur
Evelyn
Elmer

Their Children
Marjorie
Lucille
Virginia,
Catherine Helen

My Parents
Arthur Tolf
Catherine Helen Kelly

Their Children
Lenore
Katherine
Myra
Gale
Claire
Francine

❖PART ONE❖

The House I Remember

The six Tolf girls, circa 1961. From left: Gale, Myra, Claire, Francine, Lenore, and Katherine.

BIRTHDAY

I was born at Silver Cross Hospital in Joliet, Illinois, on July 10, 1958. Three years earlier, *Look Magazine* named my hometown one of eleven "all American cities." This must have pleased the folks of Joliet, because it had never quite shaken its reputation as a prison town. Little wonder. The State Prison, built from yellow limestone quarried on its own site, was a grim castle on North Collins Street. Stateville Penitentiary, which housed the infamous child killers Leopold and Loeb earlier in the century, and would incarcerate criminals like Richard Speck and John Wayne Gacy later, lay five miles northwest of it.

Both institutions employed a respectable number of townspeople, but less than Caterpillar Tractor. In fact, Joliet's largest employer in the 1950s was the Elgin, Joliet and Eastern rail line that everyone called "the J." Thousands of locals, including my aunts Ginny and Evie, worked in the J's many offices and machine shops. Then there was "the Works": three former steel-producing sites located on the east, north and south borders of Joliet. It's claimed that air pollution can create especially vibrant sunsets. I remember decadent orange and yellow skies with Joliet's southern smokestacks silhouetted against the blaze. Factory towers stamped against sunsets are stenciled in my memory, like Jefferson Street Bridge and the black water of the canal. But I'm getting ahead of myself.

On this particular afternoon, worlds away from the grit of steel and limestone, I imagine my mother, Helen Kelly Tolf, lying in the sunny bed of a peaceful maternity ward at Silver Cross Hospital, cradling me, her sixth daughter. Smiling down at her is my father, Arthur Tolf, clutching a bouquet of flowers that my two oldest sisters helped choose. Or maybe he's carrying peonies wrapped in damp newspaper and is wearing his one good suit for this visit. It's strange to think of my mother and father, younger than I am as I write this, alive and important to each other, while I have barely entered their lives. I felt the same jolt of surprise when I looked at my birth certificate and saw my parents' histories typed in boxes as if they were just *anyone*: NAME, ARTHUR CLARENCE TOLF; RACE, WHITE; AGE, 43, BIRTHPLACE, JOLIET, ILLINOIS. MAIDEN NAME, HELEN CATHRYN— they misspelled it—KELLY; RACE, WHITE; AGE, 40; BIRTHPLACE, JOLIET, ILLINOIS.

My parents soon took me home to a quiet neighborhood on Joliet's West Side, blocks from where my mother herself was raised. Dutch elm disease hadn't yet ravaged the area, so fifty-year-old elm trees still formed a green canopy over Willow Avenue. The Lee Theater, where I saw Walt Disney's *Summer Magic* five years later, stood on the corner of Raynor and Jefferson, not far from a National Grocery. Further west on Jefferson, next to a cornfield, was a tiny red and white drive-in called McDonald's.

Arthur and Helen Tolf had lived at 206 South Raynor Avenue for two years. Before that, they lived on rural New Lenox Road. Mom picked raspberries from bushes that grew in her own backyard and waved to her neighbor, Mrs. Cavenetti, who was in her seventies. If Mrs. Cavenetti had an argument with her husband on Saturday night, she walked haughtily along the side of the road to High Mass the next morning in a long black dress as her husband drove beside her, alternately pleading and shouting in Italian.

As for how my parents got along, I have a box of notes that Dad used to write to his wife on the backs of check deposits, receipts, napkins. "Darling Helen," says one, "You are the loveliest girl in the world, and I am the luckiest man."

Baby doll, I will
love you forever.
A

Dearest Helen,
I wanted to marry you the first night
I took you out.
A

There is only one
Helen Kelly.
Always,
A

There are dozens of these notes on small squares of paper, brown and brittle now, gathered in a cloth bag nestled in the drawer of my desk. My mother must have saved every one.

Helen and Arthur, 1947-1948—the first year of their marriage.

As much as my parents loved New Lenox Road, their quarters grew cramped. When Mom became pregnant with her fifth baby, they began looking for a larger house on Joliet's less developed, less expensive West Side. They found it on 206 South Raynor: a two-story box with a sunroom, a fireplace, four badly needed bedrooms, and one bathroom.

I was the only Tolf girl conceived in this new house, and I was the only one born at Silver Cross Hospital. Good Catholic that she was, Mom gave birth to my five older sisters at St. Joseph's, the old brick hospital on Broadway Street. But my mother had a terrible experience at St. Joseph's with Claire. After her water broke and Dad drove her to the hospital, the staff immediately tried to get hold of Helen Tolf's doctor. They could not, but two crisply-capped maternity nurses insisted that my mother put off having a baby until he came. My mother had given birth to four babies prior to this. Raw instinct shouted it was time to push, but the nurses forced her to cross her legs.

"I don't remember what I said, but I was screaming at the top of my lungs," my mother told me later, when I was attending the College of Saint Francis, a small liberal arts college located in Joliet. Dressed in flannel night gowns and robes, we talked together in the kitchen at night after Dad went to bed.

"Why didn't you sue them, Mom? Those horrible nurses!"

My mother poured herself some more Carlo Rossi blush wine, which she drank over ice cubes, and lit a Virginia Slim cigarette, offering one to me as well. Back then, I too smoked.

"Oh, honey, it was a different era. You didn't think of suing. Anyway, I never heard a man as angry as Dr. Gardener was when he finally burst into that room. He *literally* gave them hell!" (All her life, my mother misused the word "literally," a habit that never failed to annoy me when I was young enough to think it my duty to correct her—which I probably did that evening.)

If my father ever longed for a son, he never said so. Some might think this odd, but Dad was nothing if not opinionated, and I never doubted the sincerity of his opinions. "Your mother and I were happy to take whatever babies God gave us. *Whatever* babies. If He'd have given us more, we'd have taken more! Do you know what I call married couples who don't want children? Selfish! All they care about is their fine homes and fancy vacations." My father expressed this sentiment frequently throughout my childhood. He also insisted that working for yourself was best.

Dad did not earn a steady paycheck at Caterpillar or the J. Instead, he was a piano tuner. He tuned pianos all over the Joliet area, from Channahon to Frankfort to a sleepy little farming community called Naperville. Dad also sold pianos. At first, he sold them out of the garage behind 206 South Raynor. But his next-door neighbor, Charlie Merlow—a name that to this day is synonymous for me with a troublemaking, no-good busybody—complained to the police about it. My parents had to find space to rent. By the time I was born, they had a small store on Bluff Street near what in earlier times had been the business center of Joliet. A decade later, Bluff Street's historic Merchant Row was razed to make room for low-income housing. But on July 10, 1958, Art Tolf's piano store, with its homemade curtains and hand-painted sign, overlooked the canal and downtown Joliet.

I don't know if my mother particularly wanted a piano store or how much she worried over her husband's undependable income. But I do know that she loved her Arthur and refused to let anyone criticize him in front of her. All of their lives, my parents formed a united front to the rest of the world although in many ways they were opposites. Dad was a doer while Mom was a thinker, a reader. They didn't marry until after my father came back from World War II, but Arthur Tolf knew who Helen Kelly was in high school. "A tall, skinny good-looking girl who was always carrying around a stack of books. Crimany, the books your mother carried around! I think they weighed more than she did."

My father always chuckled at this memory. But he never laughed about the relics and indulgences that in 1958 were still very much part of his wife's Catholic Church.

"A scapular around your neck is not going to get you into heaven! And paying the priests to say Mass for you after you're gone isn't going to, either! Pagan!"

Dad was born a Baptist and never stopped being one, even though he converted to Catholicism—less for my mother's sake, I think, than because he knew it would upset his father. Every Sunday, Art Tolf ushered at St. Patrick's Sunday Mass. But after returning home to a plate of bacon and eggs and a can of beer, Dad attended his real service. In the sunroom which served as his study, he listened to the sermon of Preston Bradley that he had recorded on his big tape recorder. Preston Bradley, Reverend of the People's Church in Chicago, was one of Dad's heroes. Often Bradley's words, always wise and always uplifting, brought tears to my father's eyes.

After the trauma my mother experienced while in labor with Claire at St. Joseph's Hospital, she became badly depressed. She never used these words when she described her emotional state, but she must have been. Dad spent more time holding and cuddling the new baby than Mom did. How I know this, I don't remember—but it makes sense. Dad bonded with Claire as he bonded with no other daughter, and to this day, my sister Claire sees no wrong in our father.

Eventually, my mother saw a psychiatrist—something few housewives in Joliet did in 1956. Since my parents' financial situation was always a bit rocky, I am guessing it was my Aunt Marjorie who paid the psychiatrist's bill. And I'll bet it was Marjorie who insisted her youngest sister get some help around the house, which came in the form of two black sisters from the East Side, Luella and Pruella. (I don't remember either sister, but I know one of them screamed to sweet Jesus when she reached under the couch for a toy that had rolled there and instead grabbed a live turtle.)

Aunt Marjorie adored my mother. "You're a pretty girl, Katherine," she once told my second oldest sister, who wanted to be an actress, "but you can't hold a candle to your mother when she was your age." Marjorie told Katherine that when Mom was in high school, some form of test—"IQ, but more than that"—had been administered to the entire student body. Helen Kelly ranked in the genius level and was tracked for subsequent years. Mom's oldest sister never once said a disloyal word about Arthur Tolf, but I suspect she believed her precious Helen had "married below her station."

Mom had three sisters. Marjorie, a school teacher, was the oldest. She rented a roomy second-floor apartment on Hickory Street and took care of Papa, my grandfather. My only memory of Papa is a framed black-and-white photograph that Mom kept on her dresser of an old man with a stern expression and Teddy Roosevelt glasses. But I learned at a young age that Mom and her three sisters idolized this portly, white-haired man. Papa raised them as a widower during the Depression, working as a guard at Stateville Penitentiary. I loved listening to Mom's stories about him.

"I barely remember my mother—I had just turned seven when she died. Her death was much harder on Margie. Margie tried to take on so much at only fourteen! But, oh, I remember missing my mother terribly one morning. I refused to get out of bed, I refused to eat. I was in that bed for days. Margie told me later that she and Papa were on the brink of taking me to the hospital. One day, Papa sat down next to me. 'Helen,' Papa said, 'what is it? Tell me what I can do.' I told him I wanted my mother back. Poor Papa! He didn't say anything for the longest time. Finally, he told me he couldn't bring my mother back, but he'd get me anything else if I would only eat a little something."

We would have been in the kitchen again, Mom and I. A lit candle on the table might have flickered upon my mother's face, making her look pretty and girlish as she shook her head, laughing. "I was a practical child. I knew I would probably never get this chance again. So I thought about it very seriously. 'Papa,' I told him, 'I'll try to get better if you bring me a fountain pen and a pair of roller skates.' Frannie, I don't know how he did it. Papa was always robbing Peter to pay Paul. But that evening, my father came home with the most beautiful gold fountain pen I'd ever seen—and a brand new pair of skates."

It wasn't until I was well into adulthood that I learned that my father had a very different view of Papa. "Always with the rosary, praying, praying, while Marjorie cooked and cleaned and brought him his hot milk and tucked in his blanket . . ." Dad believed Papa took advantage of his daughters, especially Marjorie. It was his opinion that after Mike Kelly stopped working at Stateville, he never even *tried* to get a job. Why should he when he had his oldest girl to support him? Naturally, Dad never shared these thoughts with his wife.

Dad, too, had family in Joliet, but he wasn't close to them the way Mom was close to her sisters. My father grew up on the East Side of town in a house built by his own father, a skilled carpenter. Dad had three brothers and one sister, but he seldom talked about his siblings or his parents. When he did, it was often with a trace of bitterness. My father got along pretty well with the middle brother, Albert, but he believed his father favored Rueben, the oldest. He spoke with contempt of how Pa and Rueben would go down to the basement together to have shots of brandy. "Hypocritical is what I call that! Sneaking down to the basement like little boys. If you're going to drink, do it where people can see you." Dad also despised how Pa babied Elmer, the youngest. He and Elmer couldn't be in the same room for very long.

Prickly at best is how I'd describe my father's relationship with his one sister. Evie still lived in the house where she and her brothers had grown up; the parents' will stipulated that the house was not to be sold until their daughter chose to move. She was extremely proud of her Swedish heritage and found it slightly shocking that her brother Arthur considered America, not Sweden, his true home. Aunt Evie was also a devout Baptist who believed Jesus provided her with Signs. "I never make a decision without asking the Lord. I knew when to buy my last car because of the Lord. Jesus, I said, if the next car that passes my house is not black, I will know you are telling me to buy a new car. And do you know, the next car that passed was not black." Evie would then smile a smile as tranquil as one carved on a statue of the Buddha. "Jesus always answers me."

Hearing his sister relate this at a holiday dinner table in her quavering voice always made my father a little crazy. My mother would quickly change the subject or tell a joke—badly, I'm afraid—and laugh heartily, even if no one else did.

My four oldest sisters, 1956. From left: Lenore, Gale, Katherine, and Myra.

At forty-three, my father was no longer the slender soldier whose good looks astonished me when as a teenager I perused old photo albums from his army days. But Arthur Tolf still had bright blue eyes, and I am sure that when he gazed down at mother and baby on my birthday, he saw the same dark-haired beauty he admired from his high school days. How happy they both must have been for Mom's easy birth. Marjorie was probably babysitting the five little girls who were waiting to meet their new sister. Lenore Anne, the oldest, was eight; Katherine Mary was seven; Myra Jane was five; Gale Maureen was four; and Claire Elizabeth was two.

My mother chose their names as she chose mine, Francine Marie, not because they were in the family, but because she liked them. She had only a few blurred memories of her own mother. Other than Marjorie, seven years her senior, Helen Kelly Tolf had no motherly role model to emulate. She had to learn on her own how to calm babies, discipline toddlers, nurture little girls.

I remember playing dolls in the attic with Claire when I was perhaps seven or eight. Searching for a box of doll dishes, we came across some dusty books by a serious looking man wearing big black glasses. Inside were pages and pages of boring words and boring photographs of infants in playpens, infants in high chairs, mothers holding infants. We asked our mother about the books. She explained that when our older sisters were little babies, she needed to learn how to take care of them in the best way possible; this man, Dr. Spock, had helped her a great deal. How odd to learn that Mama had read books about how to take care of us. She knew exactly how to take care of us!

The year I was born, a gallon of milk cost a dollar at the National Grocery, a postage stamp was four cents, and I-80 hadn't yet sliced through the southern tip of our town. In 1958, fifty-year-old roads still connected Joliet to her neighbors. Two and a half blocks from my parents' house, seven Masses, all of them in Latin, were said every Sunday at St. Patrick's Church on Marion Street. The Church's grade school, where three of my sisters would attend that fall, had eight hundred students and eighteen teachers. And the maple tree that rose above our roof by the time I left home was a sapling.

July 10 was a Thursday, so according to the "Monday's Child" rhyme, I had far to go. I am still learning how true this is, but I have my mother to guide me. Not a day passes that I don't think about Helen Kelly Tolf. I cannot imagine navigating the terrors and heartaches of childhood and adolescence without such an anchor. I remember her voice, a low-pitched chime. I remember her delight in the beautiful. My mother's birthday was January 29, 1918. This means the woman holding me in her arms in that bright maternity ward at Silver Cross Hospital was Tuesday's Child—a child full of grace.

Helen Kelly, June, 1947—four months before her wedding.

THAT SISTER

Lenore

Who had to do everything first. Who fought over curfews and defended a pair of black bikini panties my father found in the dryer when she was seventeen. Who liked Motown better than Rock and devoured movie magazines instead of literature. The sister who tried to sneak out of the house wearing Gale's new platform heels, fell while running for the door, and faked a broken ankle as Gale tried to yank the shoes off her feet. Daydreamer in high school, Miss Agriculture at Joliet Junior College, graduate student in educational counseling. Named for the Edgar Allen Poe poem that begins, *Ah, broken is the golden bowl.* Lenore of the hourglass figure who loved Franksville Foot-longs and Twinkies and didn't need Jane Austen. So sexy at twenty-two in low-cut jeans and a halter top, I am stunned when I find the 1972 photograph.

Katherine

Who added glamour to backyard cookouts just by being there. Who posed for the camera at three, was in Little Theater at ten, and starred in a college production of *The Owl and the Pussy Cat* at twenty. Katherine, who cut jelly sandwiches into restaurant triangles and surprised me with a poison ring I longed for when I was nine. Who steamed her face without removing her contacts so they stuck to her eyes, and who insisted in agony that she would *not* wear the white shorts to the emergency room because they made her look fat. Sister who slammed doors most passionately and gave the best presents. Who was photographed by Victor Skrebnesky and could still be a model. Katherine, who sent me a rose-colored linen dress for my first poetry reading, along with a card that informed me in crisp handwriting that I would be brilliant—and for god sake to wear heels.

Myra

Who was Mimoo to me before she was Myra. The sister who taught school to neighborhood kids and gave them piano lessons. Sister of freckles and jokes, prettiest baby, most cherishable toddler. Myra who held my hand when we crossed Jefferson Street Bridge to go downtown because I was scared I would fall into the canal's black water. The sister who could coax Dad into a good mood and performed a hilarious chicken walk for Claire and me if we begged hard enough. Myra, who vamped in front of her bedroom mirror to Elvis Presley's *Let Yourself Go,* who was crazy about Sidney Poitier and Joe Namath and making people laugh. No scenes or drama, the middle sister, the amiable one. Myra who went to the prom with a boy who was ridiculed because she could not bear to hurt his feelings. Who never told anyone, at sixteen, how difficult that kindness was.

Gale

The other middle sister. The only one of us who had an imaginary friend when she was small and liked angel food cake better than chocolate. Little nun in the photograph who kneels in prayer, a white towel draped over her head, as her three older sisters grin for the camera. Gale who made up adventure games to be acted out and delighted in finding patches of violets and lilies of the valley. Who learned embroidery from Mrs. White and drawing from no one, fairies and mermaids blooming effortlessly on the page by the time she was in kindergarten. The sister who wrapped her bedroom lamp in a blue nylon robe to create atmosphere and started a fire that Dad had to put out. Gale who at four wanted to be a morning glory when she grew up. Who at twenty-eight almost slipped away forever.

Claire

Who was Dodo first, best friend, bossiest teacher. Sister of the secret language we invented, sister of waltzes we danced to with imaginary princes in the Quigley's yard. Claire who stood up to the Baherlings and cared more about fairness than fitting in. The spitting image of her father, adults claimed, with her thick blond hair and her snub nose and her passion for the piano. Claire who performed an incredibly uncool dance involving high kicks whenever she was especially happy. The sister I hated and loved the fiercest, the sister who stood in front of her eighth grade class and told students they should be ashamed for the heartless trick they played on a boy who never returned to St. Patrick's after that morning's cruelty. Claire, a stilt-legged, horn-rimmed thirteen-year-old, braver that day than I could ever be.

SUPPERS

Sometimes on winter Sundays we'd have pancakes for supper. Mom had a cast iron skillet with six indented disks she poured batter into. There were eight of us, so she had to make a lot of batches. Our family ate in the kitchen, not the dining room, on pancake nights. Tina, our fat black Chihuahua, snored on a blanket in front of the register, basking in the heat from the furnace. Pancake suppers were cozy but always made me a little *blue*, a word my mother sometimes used. Maybe just the fact that I was in first grade and had school the next day. Plus, I did not think that pancakes were a proper dinner; it wasn't right to have something *sweet* for dinner.

But Sundays were when *Bonanza* was on, and there was nothing blue about that. Our whole family watched *Bonanza*, even Dad. Lenore, who was fourteen, had a crush on Adam, but the rest of us girls loved Little Joe. During the opening segment, when a map of Ponderosa County is shown on screen and begins to catch on fire around the edges, my sisters and I blew hard on the television set to make sure the map didn't burn up. If we were lucky, Dad made black or orange cows—root beer or orange pop with a scoop of vanilla ice cream—before the show.

"Orange cow or black cow?" he'd ask the next daughter in line.

"Orange cow. No, wait a minute, Daddy . . . black cow!"

"Better make up your mind, Claire. Because once I pour, *that's what you're getting.*"

Indecision irritated Dad. So did horse play. "Cut out that horse play!" he'd shout towards the living room, where Katherine and Myra were throwing sofa pillows at each other, shrieking with laughter. "You're laughing now, but you'll be crying later!" My father knew how easily girls' hilarity turned into sobs—but he was seldom able to quash the hilarity.

Normally, we ate supper in the dining room. We had a wooden table that came apart; we could put three leaves in the middle to lengthen it. We needed all three. With eight people to plan and prepare dinner for every evening, my mother's cooking was not fancy. She dumped frozen vegetables into boiling water so peas and corn came out waterlogged, and I think for the first twelve years of my life the only lettuce I ate was iceberg. But my mother cooked things like pot roast and ham just fine. She made delicious homemade beef stew and navy bean soup that simmered all afternoon in a big silver pot, along with onions, carrots, celery, and a ham hock. Claire and I hated that soup; its smell alone inspired loud and dramatic protests. "Eeooo, bean soup! We don't have to eat it, do we Mom?" I didn't realize until I was a teenager how good that soup was.

Certain foods always went together. If Mom made Polish sausage, we knew we would have it with Frank's Quality Kraut. If she made canned salmon loaf, we knew it would be served with baked creamed corn and homemade rice pudding. Dad liked that dinner. Rice pudding was the one dish my Swedish father asked my Irish mother to learn to make. Dad thought Mom was a wonderful cook. He was not a fussy man when it came to meals. As long as no blood ran from the meat and nothing was suspiciously spicy, he was happy.

He watched our table manners, however, like a hawk: an obsessive, irritable hawk. "Don't talk with your mouth full, Gale! Slow down, Frannie. Where's the fire?" My father never finished high school, but he knew the importance of good table manners and was determined that all six of his daughters would have them. One thing that bothered him more than just about anything was if we dared to eat elbow macaroni—always topped with canned tomatoes—with a spoon. On nights that we had family-pack pork chops and elbow macaroni, Dad kept careful watch. Among the clatter of silver and the chatter of six girls, he'd catch one of us cheating.

"Lenore, what's that in your hand?"

"But I can't get the juice if I use a fork!"

Mom knew this was important to Dad. "Do as your father says, Lenore."

"Fine! But Debbie Randall can't believe we all have to sit down for supper. *Her* family gets to watch TV when they eat, and they don't have to do it all together, either."

Here my father, who had been listening impatiently, would interrupt. "If this Debbie Randall jumped off Jefferson Street Bridge, would you jump, too? Do you want to know what's wrong with young people today?" We didn't; Dad had told us many times. The explanation involved jumping off the Jefferson Street Bridge and why listening to Herman's Hermits would turn our brains to mush. "They have no minds of their own! Look at the music you girls listen to. No melody. Just thump thump thump. And *why* do you listen? Because everyone else does!"

Preparing dinner for eight people involves a lot of dishes. Mom divided cleaning them into three tasks: scraping, washing and drying. All six of us took turns. Washing and drying dishes could actually be enjoyable if you did it with a sister you were getting along with. Somebody was invariably mad at somebody, but my mother knew it was *always* hopeless to assign shared tasks to Gale and Claire. They brought out the worst in each other. Gale, who was imaginative and artistic, turned into a pretentious phony around Claire. And Claire, who had a profound sense of justice, became a pompous moralist around Gale. As for Claire and me, when we weren't best friends, we were enemies. Mom would have to sit us down so each of us, too furious to spit, could tell our side of a quarrel.

Myra got along with everyone. They say middle children are peacemakers; *she* certainly was. She was also a natural-born teacher. The Christmas that I was six, Myra received a standing blackboard as one of her gifts. She was soon teaching school to Claire and me and the Baherling girls—Judy, Julie, and Mary Therese—in our basement, handing out blue and silver stars as prizes. A few years later, Myra conducted interpretive dance classes in our living room. She'd put on an album by Herb Alpert and the Tijuana Brass, a band that was very popular in the sixties, and order Julie or me to dance to "Bittersweet" or "A Taste of Honey." Away we'd flail, all elbows and knobby knees, imagining we looked like one of the Gold Diggers on the Dean Martin show. The only time we felt silly was when we had to dance to "Love Potion Number Nine" because it had a throaty-horned passage that sounded like a striptease.

"Myra, do I *have* to?" I would wail.

"You do. Pretend you're Joey Heatherton. I want a sexy pose right now."

"Promise me you're not going to laugh."

Myra would promise. But when I put my hands on my hips and pursed my lips, she wouldn't just laugh—she would *howl.* "You look—" she could hardly get the words out. "You look like you've got an awful side ache!" By then, Julie would be howling, too. But as furious as I'd get, I couldn't stay mad at Myra.

Katherine, the second oldest, usually got along with everyone too. Katherine was interested in theater from a very young age and produced her own plays when she was still in grade school. With the help of Myra and Gale and sometimes, grudgingly, Lenore, scripts were written, rehearsed, and performed in our garage. Pink ribbed bedspreads draped over a rope were our curtains. A wooden piano crate was our dressing room. Invitations were sent out around the neighborhood. And kids came: the Quigleys, the Darins, the Gavins. They paid admission and sat on the old armchairs and folding chairs and stools we rounded up and placed in rows.

Lenore didn't care about acting but was crazy about babies. She babysat for neighborhood mothers and adored a chubby, red-haired toddler everyone in our neighborhood called Ladybug. But Lenore had little use for Claire and me. If Mom and Dad went out on a Friday evening, she lorded it over us.

"*I'm* choosing the TV shows tonight. And at eight o' clock, I'm going to watch *Hogan's Heroes*."

"That's not fair! Mom promised us we could watch *Honey West!*"

"You can watch *Honey West* if you do whatever I ask. Go get me my bedroom slippers, Frannie. Claire, I want you to make me a peanut butter and jelly sandwich. "

Lenore would continue applying mascara calmly in front of a mirror she set up at the kitchen table. She and Dad fought over how much eye makeup she wore.

Claire would be shaking with righteous rage. "I'm not making you anything! I know you have cigarettes in your top dresser drawer. I'm telling Mom as soon as she comes back."

"That's right, I'm telling Mom, too!"

Now it was Lenore's turn to lose her cool. "You little brats! Keep your damn paws out of my stuff!"

"We're telling her you *swore,* too." We'd dance around Lenore until she brandished a hairbrush—then we scrambled upstairs.

As we grew older, my sisters began preparing supper on their own, aided by written instructions from Mom, who was now working full time at the piano store. No one liked it when Lenore got supper duty, but cooking came naturally to Katherine. Whereas Lenore served beans heated up from the can, Katherine added diced onions and barbecue sauce and baked them with strips of bacon across the top that were bubbling and crisp when she took the pan out of the oven. If Katherine cooked a ham, she stuck cloves in it and served it with her own mustard sauce. She was the only sister to actually use the small silver dinner bell that hung on a hook in the doorway between the kitchen and dining room.

Myra was not a fancy cook but made dishes we all liked, like Spanish Rice: ground beef, chopped onions and green peppers, canned tomatoes, and four cups of cooked Minute Rice added just before serving. She was the only daughter willing or able to cook herring for Dad. He didn't ask for it very often, but two or three times a year my father had to have his herring. It came in a wooden box encrusted in salt. You soaked the fish for an entire day in a pan in the basement, then deboned it. Myra would slice off the head and tail, split the herring in half, scoop out the guts, then carefully lift out the entire back bone.

"It looks like a scorpion," I said, eyeing the dreadful thing over my sister's shoulder one afternoon when I was perhaps eleven and Myra a junior in high school.

"Come on, it's not so bad. I dare you to touch it, Frannie."

I was gathering up courage to touch that awful backbone when my sister suddenly dangled it in front of my face. "Or maybe I'll put it down your back!" I screamed and ran up the stairs, with Tina, our Chihuahua, barking at my heels. I could feel Myra laughing right behind me until I ran into the bathroom and slammed the door. It was good that Dad wasn't home that day. We were definitely indulging in horse play.

My job was to help the assigned sister prepare supper. They let me peel vegetables, set the table, and make coffee ahead of time. If it was Gale's turn, I'd help her decorate menus for the entire family in which the various courses were described: *Appetizer: a refreshing glass of ripe tomato juice. Entre: meatloaf with Gale's secret sauce.* Gale and I would sit at the kitchen table designing borders for each menu, forgetting about the food that needed to be prepared.

Once, Mom bought expensive pork chops—not family pack, but thick—and left careful instructions on how long to cook them in the broiler. Gale decided those pork chops should be stuffed. I don't remember what the stuffing consisted of or how the meal turned out. But I can still see my sister sewing a raw pork chop with a needle she took from the red pincushion on top of Mom's dresser.

In the summer, our Aunt Margie, who lived only three blocks away, dropped by with zucchini or rhubarb from her garden and sometimes a big bunch of peonies wrapped in a damp paper towel. Mom cooked the rhubarb with frozen strawberries. It was delicious that way. She always stewed the zucchini with tomatoes. That's how Margie made it, too. When I was growing up, I thought you weren't supposed to eat zucchini without tomatoes. Once when Margie came over, she was upset over a dream she had the night before.

Lenore, when she was attending Joliet Junior College, circa 1969.

Katherine, 1964.

"I was trying to make a leg of lamb for a whole room of people," she told us. "The potatoes needed to be peeled, and I was looking all over the kitchen for my mint jelly. You girls wouldn't offer a finger to help!"

Katherine laughed. "But Margie, it was a *dream*! You can't be mad at us for how we acted in your dream."

"We never even *have* leg of lamb, Margie," added Claire.

Margie was not convinced. "Not one finger," she said sadly before leaving. "And I was near exhausted. Tell your mother I'll have some cucumbers for her soon."

Myra, 1967.

We didn't go out to eat very often. When we did, it was something to get excited about. The place we went to most often was Marishka's, a restaurant about one and a half miles north of our house, on Theodore Street. It probably took only ten minutes to get there by car, but when I was young Marishka's seemed very far away. The restaurant had three levels, like a ranch house, and was always crowded. It smelled so wonderful when I stepped inside that my stomach started growling immediately. Marishka's had red-checkered tablecloths and an enormous swordfish mounted on one of the walls. Its specialty was poor boy sandwiches. If we ordered the poor boy dinner, we got a beef sandwich made with French bread dripping with garlic butter, a double-baked

Gale, 1965.

potato with sour cream, and a salad with our choice of dressing: French, Italian or Thousand Island. Our family always ordered the poor boy dinner. Once Katherine ordered Shrimp Dijon instead. She did not consult anyone. She simply informed the waitress in a cool, grown-up voice that she would have Shrimp Dijon. My father was stunned. One would have thought Katherine, who was perhaps sixteen at the time, had just announced she was getting married.

Mom never bought certain products I saw advertised on TV, products that looked wonderful to *me*, like Rice-a-Roni and Hamburger Helper. We did not have potato chips or pop in the house. But once in a while, Mom and Dad surprised us. One evening after going out to eat by themselves—a rarity—they walked in the door with bags of hamburgers and chocolate shakes from McDonald's. All six of us were watching *Gorgo*, a horror movie about a dinosaur whose baby is stolen from her. McDonald's has never tasted as good to me as it did that night.

The last time I was together with all but one of my sisters—Gale could not make the trip—was at my Aunt Ginny's funeral. I was forty years old. Margie and Mom and Dad had already passed away. It was a terrible day, beginning with chilly politeness in church and ending with furious words exchanged in Marjorie and Ginny's bungalow, where we gathered after the ceremony. Hard to guess, that frigid afternoon, that every night growing up, the five of us sat at the same table, sharing food and laughter, interrupting each other, getting yelled at by Dad for eating too fast.

Our family had fights about the Vietnam War at that dining room table. We had arguments about religion and rock music. Dad ranted about hippies whose jeans dragged in the dirt as Katherine or Lenore rolled her eyes. But every night we were *there*, together. I remember sun pouring through venetian blinds so our dining room was striped with late afternoon light. Plates stacked with corn on the cob and slices of watermelon were placed at either end of the table. Dad sat at the east end of it, Mom at the west. One of us said Grace, which began: *Bless us, oh Lord, for these thy gifts.* My father said a resounding "Amen!"

Then, not guessing it was wonderful, we had supper.

Becoming a Writer: Nine

I t was the end of a lunch hour in early May. I was standing in the sunny, blacktopped area between the Old School and the New School. My fourth-grade classroom was in the Old School, whose two ancient halls, smelling of crayons and lemon wax, flanked St. Patrick's Church. Next year, I would be in the New School. I would sit at a desk whose top lifted up, and I would get to change classrooms during the day, like a high school student.

I was feeling grown-up in my flowered shift with red trimming that matched my red shoulder-strap purse. At the age of nine, I had no need for a purse, but Mom, who I secretly still wanted to call Mama, let me carry one on those rare days we were not required to wear our green-plaid uniforms. The dress and the purse were hand-me-downs from Claire, but I didn't mind. Claire took good care of her clothes.

I noticed Trudi DiTavio and two other girls walking toward me. Trudi DiTavio was the coolest girl in fourth grade. She had light-green cat's eyes and shoulder-length brown hair that was glossy and straight like the teen models that appeared in Sears and Montgomery Ward catalogs. Trudi had never said hello to me, much less sought me out on the playground. I tried to act nonchalant when she and her two friends walked up to me, inches too close.

"Hey, look at Tolf's outfit."

Trudi's mascots tittered obediently. Their leader gave me the once-over. "It's cute. You look cute."

"Thanks! You—you do, too." Trudi was wearing a miniskirt and white go-go boots, the kind of clothes my mother would never buy for me. *Her* hair wasn't tied back with a big bow the way mine was, a bow tied and fluffed out by my mother every morning in the dining room after she brushed my blond hair until it crackled.

"Thanks!" It was a perfect imitation of how I said it. I didn't know how to react to Trudi's mimicry, so I smiled stupidly, hating her.

"Let's see your purse."

I shrugged off my almost-new red shoulder strap purse and held it out so the three girls blocking my way could get a better look at it.

Trudi's eyes were a dazzling jade because of the sun, which created diamonds in the blacktop we were standing on. She shook her head, brown bangs swinging perfectly. "No, Tolf. I mean, *give* it to me."

I hesitated just long enough for her to know I didn't want to. Then, I handed over my purse.

She unsnapped the clasp and began removing its contents, one by one. "A pink comb. A Holy Card. Hey, look, Tolf has a hanky, with a bunch of cherries embroidered in one corner. Ooh, how sweet! Did your mommy give it to you?"

As a matter of fact, my mother *had* given me that lace-trimmed hanky, along with a blue quilted-satin hanky box. My mother was older than most mothers. She called me Francine Marie as if it were the most beautiful name in the world. She gave me gifts that were not cool but were wonderful. I made what I hoped was a pained look. "Yeah. I carry it around so I won't hurt her feelings."

After a few more comments, a few more titters, the examination that bright day more than forty years ago was over. Trudi thrust hanky and comb and whatever else I had back into my purse. She was bored with this game. I was hugely relieved I was not carrying anything too embarrassing. Relieved the most popular girl in our fourth grade class did not make a bigger deal about the hanky with cherries on it.

If she had scrawled with a ballpoint pen on that precious hanky, then let it flutter to the blacktop, all the while watching me with those dazzling jade-green eyes, would I have called her a bitch, given her a bloody nose? I want to say yes, but that wasn't what happened. Not in grammar school. Not in high school.

I smiled wider. I hated deeper.

THE AUNTS

My mother had three sisters who seemed to hover over my childhood like three unlikely fairy godmothers. Margie was the plump pink-faced one who taught Language Arts at Hufford Junior High. She was a second mother to us, especially to my older sisters. Margie was cheerful and generous and always involved with a project, whether it was taking Misty, her gentle Weimaraner, to obedience school, or setting up a dark room in her well-scrubbed basement. Every December, Margie took us to Marshall Field's Department Store in Chicago to see the window decorations and have tea in the Walnut Room. In the summer, we went to Oak Brook Shopping Center to eat at Henrici's— a restaurant that had red velvet wallpaper and French pastries for dessert— and walk through the outdoor mall's landscaped gardens and fountains.

Ginny, who lived with Margie, was taller and less sunny-natured than her older sister. "Cripes, Maria, take off those boots!" were the first words out of her mouth when my sisters and I came over at Christmas. I was six when I mustered the courage to ask Ginny why she never married. "Never married?" my aunt snorted, lighting up a Pall Mall. "I was married for ten years. Whatsa matter with you? Don't you remember Ang?" Since Angelo died when I was two, the answer would have been no. I knew this was not a good enough excuse for Aunt Ginny.

Lucille was the aunt who did not live in Joliet but in Barrington, which had woods and private beaches and houses that looked like they belonged on the cover of *Architecture Digest*. She and her husband, Uncle Al, lived in such a house. It had three balconies and three bathrooms, facts that impressed me deeply when we visited once a year at Thanksgiving. Lucille was flashier than her sisters. She bleached her hair platinum blond and favored bright red lipstick I could taste when she kissed me on holidays. I dreaded being kissed on the mouth by my Aunt Lucille, but I loved the fancy soaps and guest towels in her bathrooms.

Margie, born in 1910, was eight years older than my mother, the same amount of years that separates me from my oldest sister, Lenore. But there the similarity ends, for when her own mother died, Marjorie, who was only fourteen, became a surrogate mother to her three sisters. It was a role she would play her entire life.

"Papa never wanted Marjorie to assume so much responsibility," my mother told me one summer evening when we were sitting in lawn chairs at the side of the house sipping iced tea. "He knew she was only two years older than Lucille. He wanted her to enjoy her teenage years. But Marjorie's deeply stubborn. You can*not* tell her what to do." Mom let out a sigh: pure love, pure exasperation. "Marjorie Kelly, who always knows what's best. But what a big heart! I remember being in high school and wanting a white woolen coat more than anything in the world. I asked Margie if we could possibly afford it. She said no, and she was right. 'Helen,' she said, 'it's too expensive, and it's impractical. A navy coat would last much longer.' But Frannie, about a month later, she surprised me with that coat. She must have worked a second job to buy it." My mother smiled, remembering the moment as we breathed in the scent of privet from the bush blooming underneath the kitchen window. "That's Marjorie."

I think when Mom was growing up, Lucille, not Marjorie, was like the oldest sister and Virginia—or Ginny as she was called—was her best friend. She and Ginny remained close as they grew older. When my mother married Arthur Tolf, a soldier home from World War II, Miss Virginia Kelly was her maid of honor. According to the *Joliet Herald News*, Ginny wore a royal blue velveteen dress and a half-hat trimmed with matching feathers. With her pert smile and curly eye lashes, my aunt must have looked fetching indeed, but although she "had her chances," as they say, she was content with her office job at "the J"—the Elgin, Joliet and Eastern rail line—and her quiet life on Hickory Street with Papa and Marjorie. It took Angelo Pellegrini to persuade Ginny to leave that safe niche. She was thirty-five when she married him.

Marjorie and Virginia Kelly, circa 1950.

Angelo had married twice before, although not in the Catholic Church. I know from the process of osmosis—the way family stories sink into memory, so they seem a collection of scenarios you took part in—that he played cards, enjoyed nights on the town, and drank. What's more, he was extraordinarily handsome, with a luxurious baritone and a magnetism that drew women *and* men. Both Mom and Dad liked Ang tremendously; he came to our house often.

If my father wasn't around to share a beer with, Ang chatted in the kitchen with Mom, the newest baby gurgling on his lap. Lenore or Katherine tugged at his trousers for attention while my mother chopped up a chicken or snapped beans. Ang used to tell Mom how good it felt to be in a house where everything wasn't polished and dusted and exactly in its place. That, I think, is as disloyal as he ever was to his wife. I imagine my uncle, with his screen idol good looks, relaxed and happy, sun from the window lighting my mother's face. It's occurred to me that he might have been a little in love with Mom. When I suggested that teasingly to her once, she was shocked. Angelo, she said, loved *Ginny*.

"And Ginny loved Ang. There was never any question about that. But Virginia . . ." My mother paused, trying to puzzle it out for herself. "Virginia just wasn't prepared for what marriage between a man and a woman *involved*. I tried to help. I took her shopping a couple of times. 'Ginny,' I said, 'you ought to buy yourself some pretty nightgowns. Maybe some silk stockings.'"

They would probably have gone to Kline's Department Store in downtown Joliet, two dark-haired, attractive women in their mid-

Angelo Pellegrini, 1957.

thirties, strolling through what was then called the "foundations department." I can see Mom giving her sister an impetuous hug in the middle of Ginny's fretting over unwashed breakfast dishes. "Don't worry about the dishes, honey! Look at this red robe. You'd look so pretty in it. Why don't you treat yourself?"

Maybe Ginny did. Maybe in spite of any misgivings she might have had about intimacy, she and Ang shared moments of intense sweetness. They had ten years together. He died of complications following a gallbladder operation. Mom learned about Angelo's death after Ginny burst into our house, hysterical. Never before nor since had my mother seen her then forty-five-year-old sister in that state, laughing and crying at the same time, rocking herself like a child in a kitchen chair. "Oh, Ang!" she kept saying, "Oh, Ang!"

That's when Ginny moved in with Margie. First they lived in a small white house on Frederick Street, then in a brick bungalow on Hunter, three and a half blocks from our gray-shingled house on Raynor. Ginny had never learned to drive. Now Margie took her to work instead of Angelo. Although they constantly bickered—Margie was always after Ginny to clear clutter from her bedroom, and Ginny complained to Mom of her older sister's bossiness—both women enjoyed their sparring but deeply affectionate relationship.

As we girls grew older, Margie was much more involved than Ginny was in our day-to-day lives, driving us to music lessons and rehearsals, organizing summer road trips, dropping by regularly to chat with Mom about the new principal at Hufford Junior High or the shenanigans of the Charley boys who lived east of her. Ginny was private. She liked the comfort of her daily routine, which included working as a secretary at City Hall, reading a stack of newspapers every week, and watching a TV show called *The Fugitive*. But in spite of their differences, both Margie and Ginny were familiar, a part of my family and a part of the Joliet I grew up in.

Lucille was different. My mother would have quickly denied that she was the least bit defensive around Lucille, just as Lucille would have denied she was even slightly ostentatious around her younger sister. My father was less hesitant to criticize our one pair of wealthy relatives. "Al Bradish may think he's impressive, but he doesn't impress *me*. I don't care how many cars he has or what clubs he belongs to. Did you notice the wine they served us tonight? Cold Duck—cheap stuff. Do you think Albert Bradish serves Cold Duck to *his* friends?"

Mom let Dad talk on this way as we drove home from Thanksgiving dinner in velvety darkness. An old plaid blanket covered me and Claire, who were supposed to be sleeping in the back seat of our station wagon. Yet when I was older and my mother reminisced in the kitchen about her childhood and teenaged years, the Lucille she described was flamboyant and likeable. "She had the boys buzzing around her in high school, *that* I can tell you. Oh, how that girl worried Papa! But she always told him, 'I have a level head, Papa. It may be a little blonder than the good Lord intended, but it's level.'"

My favorite Lucille story concerns Aunt Nan, who invited her four motherless nieces over to dinner every Sunday—which *sounds* neighborly. In fact, Aunt Nan made it a point to treat the girls as poor relatives. Each Sunday, she set a plate of fresh butter on the table for herself and her husband. Nan slathered butter on biscuits and potatoes as her nieces, who were forbidden to partake, watched. One Sunday, twelve-year-old Lucille asked her aunt to pass the plate of butter. "Aunt Nan gave my sister a look that would have wilted any of the rest of us. But Lucille shot her the same look right back. It felt for a few seconds like a dual was going to take place at that table. But it was Aunt Nan who backed down. After that, we always helped ourselves to whatever was served!"

Not all of my mother's stories were charming. Before she married Al Bradish, when she was still in her twenties, Lucille began a ten-year affair with a married man. "He was a doctor, well respected, wealthy. Year after year, Lucille convinced herself that he would end his marriage for her. She was such a beautiful young woman, Frannie, and a wonderful nurse. She simply could not see that man for what he was."

Lucille's affair ended with an abortion. Her lover, the doctor, arranged it. She lost a dangerous amount of blood during the operation—which was performed, of course, in secret. "It was a terrible, terrible couple of days," my mother said quietly. "It nearly killed Papa."

I can't help wondering if my mother blamed Lucille for the toll that abortion took on her father. I don't want to think she did, because it seems so rigid, so judgmental. Then I consider the blame that has been cast and carried among me and my own sisters. I know how muddied a once clear family spring can become, how impossible to determine exactly how it got that way, who was right and who was wrong.

And I could be mistaken. Maybe Mom felt no

My Aunt Lucille, circa 1955.

blame at all towards her sister, only sadness. Maybe the rift between my mother and my Aunt Lucille—for there was most certainly a rift— occurred later, after she married, moved to Barrington, and joined a new set of friends, people who drank cocktails at five in the afternoon and took yearly trips to Europe. Women who owned mink coats, whose children did not wear holiday dresses from Montgomery Ward.

Yet as a child, I could not help but like Lucille. She was bright and brash and fun. I knew as the youngest of six girls that she was more interested in spending time with my older sisters than she was with me. So were Margie and Ginny. I understood. Except with my mother, I was often tongue tied around adults. I preferred to observe.

Mom and Margie took turns hosting Christmas dinners. As much as I adored my mother, I will admit here and now that Margie was the superior cook. When we went over to her house for Christmas, the whole bungalow smelled delicious. Marjorie's twenty-pound turkeys were succulent, her homemade stuffing moist, her giblet gravy, served in a gold-rimmed gravy boat and poured into hollows of creamy mashed potatoes, perfection. There were sweet potatoes with marshmallows on top, steamed rutabaga with melted butter. Ginny, second in command, always made a green-bean casserole whose ingredients included french-fried onions and a can of Campbell's cream of celery soup.

Mom and Dad drove, but when I was growing up, I'd walk over to 6 South Hunter with one or two sisters. After placing our coats across Margie's bed, we'd pick a chair to perch on in the living room. The door-bell chimed and boots stomped on the floor of the screened-in porch as more family members arrived. A card table set up in the living room held the relish tray: scalloped cucumbers, rose radishes, a glass bowl heaped with sour cream. Katherine slipped the score from *Paint Your Wagon* or *Camelot* into the door of Margie's hi-fi. She said music added atmosphere.

It always took more than one "Dinner time!" to get everyone from the living room to the dining room where the table, made longer by leaves, gleamed with china and sterling silver. Plates of oven-warmed dinner rolls and crown-shaped Jell-O molds were at either end, but Margie brought out hot dishes from the kitchen herself. As mashed potatoes and stuffing and white meat and dark meat made their way around the table, along with murmurs of, "Be careful, it's heavy," and, "Hold both ends! The gravy's dripping!" my eldest aunt supervised, her face flushed a deep rose.

"Marjorie, you outdid yourself this year," Mom would say from the far end of the room. "Why don't you sit down and eat?"

A chorus of, "Yes, Margie, sit down and relax!" always followed, to no avail. Beaming in her holiday apron, she'd ask if the turkey wasn't a little dry or the cranberries too sweet. Eventually, she'd ease into a folding chair close to the kitchen and join in the general conversation. This could concern the 1974 Watergate hearings, the new mall they were talking about building on Jefferson Street, or how Father Ryan, a big man already, was putting on the weight. Margie might offer a cheer-fully rambling explanation of why she decided to go with a frozen turkey rather than a fresh one this year, ending with, "Oh! Now I know what I wanted to say. I saw Jay Charley at Honiotos Grocery."

"Cripes, I was glad when the Charleys moved." This from Ginny, who was cleaning a wine stain off of the white table cloth with a dampened napkin and determined frown. "Those boys ran wild. The mother never could control them."

"Now, Virginia, he was very friendly. 'Miss Kelly,' he said, 'I want to wish you and yours a happy holiday.' You would never have guessed what a hellion he was."

"Jay Charley pulled the fire alarm in third grade. Sister Michael Adele made him stand in a garbage can."

"You pull a fire alarm, that's nothing to laugh about!" I can hear Dad saying above the laughter my sister Gale's remark started. "No one would have pulled any fire alarms in Daisy Reem's class." (Daisy Reem was a teacher my father had in sixth grade; I can only hope she guessed what an impression she made on one tall blond boy.) "It all comes down to family. That's what this country's built on, and it's going downhill fast."

"Arter, Arter, it's a holiday," Mom would break in, trying to keep conversation light. She knew if the Breakdown of the American Family was Dad's choice of topic that remarks about Republicans (Uncle Al was a Republican) were sure to follow. "Ginny, I saw a cardinal outside your bedroom window. Have you had a lot of birds this winter?"

"I'd have more if the damned squirrels didn't eat up my seed. I haven't been able to fill up the feeders for a while, Helen. It's too icy. I said a prayer to Saint Francis yesterday morning before going outside. Took one step onto the back porch and nearly fell down the stairs. *Thanks a lot, Saint Francis,* I said. *Get somebody else to risk their neck for your birds!*"

I never said much at holiday dinners. I was content to listen, to allow the talk and laughter sink comfortably into a sweet sense of belonging. I knew that my Aunt Margie's dining room was exactly the right place for me to be, with family and relatives at the table and Margie's oval fish platter—the one with the beautiful Chinese goldfish painted on it—on the second shelf of the china cabinet, and the oil painting of Pilcher Park hung above the mantle in her living room.

After lemon chiffon cake and rainbow sherbet was served, we stayed at the table, the candles still lit, and continued to talk. One Christmas, Lucille and my sisters and I played Spoons, a card game that is the equivalent of musical chairs. When a player draws the right combination of cards, she yells "Spoons!" and everyone dives for the pile of spoons—totaling one less than the number of players—that sits in the middle of the table. My aunt played the game as earnestly as us girls, lunging so fiercely for a spoon that her chair toppled backward, and we saw, for a harrowing moment, a girdle, two plump legs, and a pair of high heeled feet pointing at the ceiling.

Lucille died of lung cancer when I was in my early twenties. She was a widow then and spent almost every weekend at Margie and Ginny's house. The three aging Kelly girls—my three aunts—attended Sunday Mass at St. Patrick's and went out to brunch when Lucille was still well enough to do so. Then she grew worse. Late one Saturday night, Margie called Mom. It was time to say good-bye to her sister.

I don't know what my mother said to Lucille as she sat with her in Margie's bedroom. I remember she claimed Lucille gave her a beautiful smile. Mom never alluded to any friction that existed between her and her sister, the spirited twelve-year-old who refused to be treated as a poor relative—yet served her own family wine she would never have put on the table for friends. Nor did my mother ever admit that she was hurt upon finding out that Lucille left everything she had to Margie and to Ginny. Not a dime of Lucille's money was willed to her youngest sister.

I am so grateful that issue never came between Mom and Margie and Ginny. For the rest of their lives, they maintained loving and supportive relationships. Marjorie was the first to pass away. She died in her sleep at St. Joseph's Hospital in October of 1996, two days after being admitted for leg pains. Although she was eighty-six years old and a borderline diabetic, Margie was as active as anyone her age could be. Her death stunned Ginny—who still, I think, regarded her older sister as a surrogate mother.

The four Kelly girls, circa 1978. From left: Marjorie, Virginia, Helen, Lucille.

Dad had died the previous May, after months of being bedrid-den. Although Margie's death was an irreparable blow, Mom did what she could now to help Ginny, who used oxygen to aid her breathing. My mother came over daily to help her older sister perform simple chores and go through shoeboxes of paperwork that covered the dining room table. I remember Mom's frustration during phone conversations as she told me how Ginny refused to have her Social Security checks deposited, or to throw away five-year-old begging letters from the Humane Society. Ginny promised to organize her affairs, just as she used to promise Margie, but the piles of envelopes on the table grew so tall they became towers for her two cats to navigate through.

On the Thanksgiving following Marjorie's death, Mom picked up two holiday meal boxes from Boston Market. She and Ginny shared a quiet afternoon together. The era of holidays celebrated by parents and aunts and all six of us Tolf girls was long over. Lenore and Myra, my two sisters who had families and lived closest to Joliet, invited Mom and Ginny to spend the day at their homes. But Lenore's five children frankly exhausted my aunt and my mother, and Mom wasn't up for driving thirty miles to Glen Ellyn. She was not well herself.

My mother died that September of 1997. By then, Ginny had sunk into a fog of forgetfulness. She passed away in Rosedale Nursing Home four months later, the last of the Kelly girls. And although she had in her possession the bulk of what Margie and Lucille had willed to her, Ginny herself had never got around to making a will. She died intestate.

Realizing

The Distance

The Easter weekend of 2003, when I was a graduate student at Kansas State University, I had a long chat on the phone with my sister, Gale. I was then forty-four, but that didn't stop Gale from trying to treat me as her baby sister. Often when we talked, she was so intent on giving me advice it was hard to squeeze a few words of my own into her monologues. But this, for once, was a real conversation. We laughed as we finished each other's sentences.

"Remember the outfits Mom and Dad would buy us for Easter? The matching coats and shoes?"

"And hats!" Gale exclaimed. "When I was in fifth grade, I had an *exquisite* straw hat with daisies. I let you borrow it, and you got magic marker all over it."

"Serves you right for always getting out of doing the dishes. Remember the baskets Mom hid that had our names on them? And how Dad would always buy Easter lilies?"

"The whole dining room smelled like lilies. And Mom would put the eggs we dyed on an oval platter with that awful fake green grass!" Gale sounded relaxed and cheerful.

"Listen," I said, "I wonder if you'd do me a favor." I asked her if she'd be willing to write down some recollections about what it was like when she came home to Joliet, Illinois, from California twenty years ago, in 1983. "I'm taking this nonfiction class, and I'm thinking I might write about it. Would that be okay?"

"Sure! I'll write you a letter."

We finished our conversation the way we always do. I told her I loved her.

"I love you too," she said quickly before hanging up.

Three days after my conversation with Gale, I received an envelope stuffed with seven pages of single-spaced type describing atrocities our parents—Helen and Arthur—had put her through as a child, as well as some secret history: *Helen joined the Marine Corps in World War II and took the side of the Nazis. After the war she was court-martialed for it and took the Fifth Amendment on everything. There were petitions going about our neighborhood that Arthur was a pedophile. I was raised with intense hatred. Helen was a slut.* Two more letters followed, neither of these typed, the handwriting increasingly disjointed and fierce, with certain words boxed: NOT WANT SEE CHILDHOOD CURED NOT.

I should have known better. When I talked to Gale, I always tried to mention happy memories about growing up. I refused to listen to her fantastic accusations. I did this because I believed that deep down, Gale knew the truth from the lies she spun. I believed she knew Mom never starved her or permitted her to be raped. I told myself she said these things for attention. She wanted to be the star victim of her group therapy sessions at Greenwood Care.

My sister's eyes are pure green and extremely intelligent. They can contain compassion and wryness. They can also contain an eerie kind of triumph, as if she's laughing at a joke she knows no one will ever understand.

I dreamed almost nightly about 206 South Raynor, the house where I spent the first twenty-two years of my life. A square, two-storied, gray-shingled house on a street where traffic became more congested as the years passed. Two Chinese elms out front. A maple tree in our backyard. It was the interior I revisited in my sleep: the kitchen, the living room, the four bedrooms. The house was always dark, and I was always uneasy. My mother often appeared in these dreams, but it was never really her, just a woman who wore her face. I envied people who could dream about loved ones who had died. I'd never been able to do that.

My childhood memories were the opposite of my dreams. I remembered sunny rooms scattered with books, toys, and piano music. Decals of butterflies and fruit decorated our kitchen, and the school projects of six daughters were tacked on a bulletin board. My mother loved flowers and had a large cut-glass bowl she filled with lilacs or peonies or phlox, depending on what was in bloom. In fall, she'd buy colorful gourds and arrange them as a centerpiece for our dining room table. Our furniture wasn't expensive, but every few years the cheap dining room chairs got reupholstered with brand-new fabric. She'd replace our kitchen curtains with brightly patterned ones from K-Mart and buy us all new bedspreads and pillows for the bedrooms we shared.

Our house was rarely neat and clean, but it seemed full of light. Mom fixed up a part of the basement with a little table and chairs and some old dressers; that was where Claire and I, the two youngest, used to play dress up. She found a second-hand desk for Gale and, with the help of my dad, hauled it up to the attic so Gale, who was talented in art, could have a space of her own to draw and paint. My mother loved *projects*. She liked fixing things. Once our orange tomcat, Pumpkin, came home covered in oil. Mom put on a pair of rubber gloves and bathed that terrified animal in our kitchen sink. Amazingly, Pumpkin did not bite or scratch her. I think he understood she just wanted to help.

Gale moved to Colorado after majoring in Art at Southern Illinois University, and from Colorado she moved with a couple of friends (cocaine dealers, she later admitted to me, although she was too naïve to know this at the time) to Monterey, California. She had always hated Joliet. She hated the fast food restaurants and used car lots that lined Jefferson Street a few blocks north of our house. She hated the dying steel mills that surrounded the town. To this day, Gale maintains that

Joliet is a blot on the face of the earth, and that its inhabitants are sit-com-watching, beer-drinking boors. When Gale left her hometown after college, she made it clear that she never wanted to come back.

Four years after she moved, family members began to get strange telephone calls from Gale. At first, the conversations were just a little off. She was unusually interested in people she hadn't seen since high school, and she was very concerned about remembering things right. Had she got hit in the head with a baseball bat when she was ten? Did Mrs. White, a kind old lady who lived on Willow Avenue, have a basement in her house? The questions became more alarming. She'd call one of my older sisters or my Aunt Margie and ask if it wasn't true that there had been a ring of Satan worshipers at Joliet Central High School—and that her former girlfriend, Janet Ramsey, was one of them. "Look it up," she'd insist. "*I know it's on public record.*"

My mother was always grateful to Julian, Gale's boyfriend at the time. Julian may have been shiftless and he was probably an alcoholic, but he recognized that something was terribly wrong with Gale, which was more than her other bohemian friends did. "She's gotta go home, Mrs. Tolf. She's pretty far gone. I don't know what to do with her." Julian used the money Mom sent him to put Gale on a plane headed for Chicago.

When my father picked Gale up at the airport, he was met by a twenty-eight-year-old woman who was five-foot-ten and weighed ninety-seven pounds. Her eyes were vacant, and she refused to talk much. Once she was home, she drummed her fingers on tables and chain-smoked. Often, she appeared to be deep in conversation with an imaginary figure. Sometimes this conversation made her smile and nod; sometimes it made her angry.

My parents were both retired, my mother from selling furniture at Montgomery Ward, and my dad from piano tuning. My father stayed out of the situation. He was a man of integrity who had worked hard all of his life, but he could be very critical, particularly of Gale, finding fault with her hair, her clothes, and her hippie friends whose patched jeans "dragged in the dirt." "You can call your friends artists, but I call them freeloaders! Freeloaders who wear the American flag on the seat of their pants!"

Gale, on the other hand, knew exactly how to irritate our father and seldom made any effort not to, whether it was airily forgetting about cleaning the good paint brushes Dad had lent her, or being only halfway packed when he showed up at her college apartment in Carbondale to help her move. "When your sister left the house where she was raised, she didn't even say good-bye to me," Dad told me once. I was surprised and touched. I never realized how much that hurt him. I remember the day Gale left Joliet. She and Dad stood stiffly next to each other on the front sidewalk. Despite Mom's efforts, neither one attempted to hug or even converse with the other.

In any event, after Gale's return to Joliet from Monterey, my mother was adamant about caring for her at home—and Dad always did what my mother asked. Dr. Juliani, the head psychiatrist at St. Joseph Hospital, was not as easy to convince. He told Mom that Gale must be admitted *immediately* to the psychiatric ward. My mother refused. Maybe part of it was guilt: guilt any mother, however loving, would suffer for the things she'd never done for her child, the thousands of ways she'd failed her. But part of it was instinct.

"Gale would have died if I put her in the hospital," Mom said to me once. She spoke the words as simple truth, without any drama or angst. "I knew this. I knew if I brought my daughter to the psychiatric ward of St. Joseph's and left her there—alone—that I would lose her."

So at the age of sixty-four, with a husband who was suffering from painful rheumatism and utterly at a loss as to how to treat his sick daughter, Mom took Gale in, determined that she was going to get better.

Years later, when I was still living and working in Chicago, I used to visit Gale at a coffee house a half a block away from Greenwood Care in Evanston, just north of Chicago. Greenwood is the facility where Gale lives and attends therapy sessions. I'd walk into the thick, smoky air of Café Espresso and see Gale drinking what was probably her fourth cup of coffee at a table cluttered with papers, tarot cards, loose tobacco, ashes, and puddles of cream. She was always thrilled to see me and eager to introduce me to any of the regulars, many of them residents of Greenwood. "Roger! Leo! This is my baby sister! Isn't she pretty? Who do you think is prettier, me or her? If you say me, I'll roll you a cigarette!" Then she'd give a cackle, pleased with her own wit.

I put myself in neutral during these visits, because if I didn't, I'd end up getting irritated over the coffee stains on Gale's dress, and how much her voice carried as she advised me on everything from poetry to relationships. "*Darling*," she'd say, letting out a huge exhale of smoke, "you've got to remember that *poetry* is *passion*. Don't be afraid to explore your wild side. You simply have to study Jung. Do you want me to give you a Tarot reading?"

I always said yes. Gale loved to study with narrowed eyes the Hanged Man and Prince of Swords to find out what awaited me, and her readings were unfailingly generous, even when I picked terrible cards: Futility, Strife, Defeat. "The cards are telling you you're too hard on yourself. See! Here's the Knight of Swords. That's Marc. You need to rely on him more. The next time I go to a Wicca gathering, I'll work a spell for both of us. But there might not be enough magic, and I come first! I'm lighting a candle for a handsome suitor. I intend to be married by the end of the year."

———————————————

When she first returned to Joliet, Gale believed she had been cursed to blindness by an artist friend of hers from Monterey who claimed to have gypsy blood. The spells and tricks Gale had to perform every day to avoid this fate were incredibly intricate. The curse was somehow connected with stars and snakes; fairies and Satan worshipers were involved as well. There were signs foretelling everything when she was a child, but she had ignored them. All this and more was explained in a thick notebook crammed with her wild, slanted handwriting. She was furious that Dr. Juliani, who initially refused to treat Gale due to his already heavy load of patients, but who eventually gave way to my mother's pleading, refused to read it. Gale hated Dr. Juliani, hated her medication, and hated our mother for forcing both upon her.

I don't know what worried Mom most in those first few months of her daughter's return: Gale's hostility, Dad's declining health, or her very real fear that Gale would set the house on fire because she refused to stop smoking in bed. I was living in Chicago at the time, working as a receptionist at an architecture firm. I spent a lot of weekends in Joliet that year. For a long time, Gale did not seem to be making any progress. If you asked her a question, you might get a monosyllabic answer two hours later—or the next day. Often, she ignored people altogether. But she liked to play scrabble, and that's what Mom and Gale and I used to do on Friday nights at the dining room table. Mom and I would keep the conversation going while Gale stared past us, drumming her fingers on the table.

"Hells bells. I've got three E's and two N's. It's not my night. And don't you laugh at me, Francine Marie."

"Sorry, Mom! I'll trade you an O for one of your E's. Have you heard from Katherine lately?"

"Your sister called last night from New York, and we had a lovely chat. Gale talked with her, too." My mother would glance at Gale, hoping in vain for some sign that she was present.

Yet when it was Gale's turn to play, she always took it. One evening, she made a word using a Y and an X and cawed in triumph. Mom came into my bedroom before I went to bed that night.

"Frannie," she whispered, elated, "this is a *red letter day!* Gale hasn't shown that much spirit all week. It's because you're here. Thank you so much, honey."

I wanted to cry when my mother, wrapped in her thick pink robe, thanked me. I am sure there were many, many moments that she wanted to cry, too. But not always.

Within a couple of months after her return home, Gale's health improved enough for her to start caring about how she looked. She began to wear red lipstick and heavy black eyeliner, raiding my mother's closet for any clothing that might suit her. One Saturday morning, Mom and I were talking in the kitchen. I don't remember what our conversation concerned, but it must have been happy because we were both smiling when we looked up and saw Gale, dressed in a lacy but tattered negligee, at the top of the landing. She was glaring at both of us.

She stomped down the stairs, stalked into the pantry, and pulled down a brownie mix from a shelf. Clattering spoon, bowl, and pan as loudly as she could, Gale made the mix, slammed the pan into the oven, gave us both a look of disgust, and went back upstairs.

Mom and I looked at each other, dumbfounded. "Sometimes, Frannie," my mother noted, stirring her coffee carefully, " you have to laugh to keep from crying." And we did laugh, until tears ran down our cheeks. Then Mom got up, turned on the oven, and set the timer.

There is no such thing as a typical case of schizophrenia. Some people experience one episode and recover completely. Others experience remissions throughout their lives. Some never recover. I can imagine how confusing it must have been for my mother to try to educate herself about so nebulous a thing, and how hurtful some of what she read must have been. Literature regarding schizophrenia published in the nineteen sixties and seventies often points to the mother as its cause. While that theory has since been discredited, when Gale returned to Joliet in 1983, there were numerous books on the subject written by doctors and "medical authorities" who took it for granted that the mother was to blame for the child's illness.

"Wasn't it hard for you to read that literature, Mom?" I asked her once. "Even if you knew it wasn't true, it must have been painful."

My mother snorted. "I paid no attention to that nonsense!" She said this with such surety it did not occur to me to doubt her. I wonder now if my mother was anywhere near as confident as she claimed.

Gale's diagnosis is hardly definite. Over more than two decades, it has been revised and reworded. She has been treated for bipolar disorder and depression. The word "narcissistic" has been tossed around. It's not *totally* inaccurate. Gale enjoys composing ten-page resumes listing her numerous accomplishments: the galleries where her work has been shown, the journals that have published her poetry. Several times a year, she compiles poems into a collection complete with an illustrated cover. These collections might include introductions that explain her philosophy of art and the spirit world, or maybe a prayer of thanks to Apollo, her personal muse, for inspiring her to new heights of creation.

I realize the vulnerability beneath such arrogance. Yet Gale is undeniably gifted. Her watercolors of mermaids and mythological figures, intricately bordered with roses and calla lilies, remind me of miniature stained-glass windows. Her poetry is uneven but glints with uncanny power. "What are your options if you're a sadist?" she asks in a poem called "Red Rose":

> If you have your wits about you,
> you study philosophy,
> play mind games and toy with people.
> Sadists are stars and create a home
> with a telescope in the wilderness . . . .

> Sometimes it simply saddens me:

> When I worked in a nursing home
> I didn't understand the old woman
> when she was dying of a broken heart
> and they offered her a pacemaker.
> Thank God I let her cry.
> Even if I didn't understand then,
> I do now.

I've always felt a bond with her. When we were kids, we used to take long walks together after school. Gale would teach me vocabulary words she'd learned in English class; sometimes we planned our weddings. We decided the perfect menu for a wedding reception consisted of pink champagne, strawberries, and angel food cake. One summer afternoon, we discovered a couple of slim books of haiku jammed in one of the crowded bookshelves in the living room. Sprawled on the floor, we read poems by Basho and Buson out loud to each other as sun slanted through blinds. A poet by the name of Issa soon became our favorite; he made us laugh with his irreverent descriptions of fleas and frogs.

"Listen, all you fleas," my sister cried dramatically, waving the book of poetry, "you can come on pilgrimage, OK / but then, *off you git!*" We rolled on the carpet, howling. I can't imagine spending such an afternoon, at ten, with anyone but Gale.

For weeks after returning to Joliet, Gale was too frail to do much physically. Gradually, she became stronger. One afternoon in September, perhaps three months after she came home, I walked with her to West Park. Like so much about Joliet, West Park had seen better days, but it held happy memories. My sisters and I had sledded and skated there when we were kids. Gale was wearing jeans that hung loosely on her emaciated frame and a bowler hat with a feather. She walked like a puppet, her thin limbs jerking forward. When we got to the park, yellow leaves floated around us like stars. It was a golden and blue day full of rasping locusts and shimmering gusts of wind. We sat on top of a graffiti-scrawled picnic table. Gale rifled through her purse, found a crumpled pack of cigarettes, and lit one. I moved away irritably.

"It's such a gorgeous day, Gale, do you have to smoke?" I heard the vicious pettiness in my voice and immediately regretted my words. Of course my sister had to smoke. Cigarettes were the one thing that got her through one more day. Gale ignored my complaint, staring straight ahead as if I weren't there. We sat in silence as she finished her cigarette. Up until that moment, I had always assumed that Gale, the real Gale, the sister who made up adventure games and drew mermaids for me when I was little, was inside this shell of a woman who had come home. It would just take a while for her to surface. But as I looked at her immobile profile, I felt a chill. *She's gone. My sister's gone, and she's never coming back.*

Years later, something made me ask Gale if she remembered that afternoon.

"I think so," she said. "Wasn't I wearing some kind of hat?"

I grabbed Gale's arm. "What about the Scrabble games? Do you remember when you and Mom and I used to play scrabble?"

"Sure! I loved those Scrabble games. They were the high point of my week."

"But you never said anything! I used to wonder if you even knew I was there."

"I was always glad when you came home. It meant a lot to me."

"I can't tell you what that means, Gale. Why didn't you say so?"

Normally, Gale was thrilled to be asked questions about herself. She was fond of pointing out the link between genius and madness and quick to suggest that she and Van Gogh had quite a bit in common. Just this once she was understated.

"Explaining how I felt took a lot of concentration. It was hard."

The six years that Gale lived with Mom and Dad were the hardest six years of their life. I couldn't have done it. When Marc and I lived in Chicago, we'd have Gale over for dinner on holidays. I loved seeing her, but it wasn't easy. Marc used to joke that we needed to lay down drop cloths, because, by the time Gale left, the table and carpet would be stained and heavily littered with ashes and tobacco. The air would be thick with stale smoke, and I'd have to check the sofa for cigarette burns. We would drive Gale back to Greenwood and give a sigh of relief as she walked inside—and that was after only a few hours with her.

Yet when I thought of what Gale had gone through, I was ashamed to complain about carpet stains. I took my mental health for granted. I didn't know what it was like to hear voices that no one else did, or to be convinced that evil spirits were plotting against me. I'd never had to wake to a cramped room at Lydia, a mental hospital in an extremely poor area south of Chicago, where Gale was committed after a bad relapse. Considering her near-catatonic state when she came home to Joliet, my sister's accomplishments—completing her Masters in Gifted Education, devoting hours daily to her art, and almost always sounding *cheerful* when I talk to her on the phone—seem little short of miraculous. But the miracle would not have occurred if it weren't for my mother.

<hr />

The last weekend I spent at 206 South Raynor was in the late spring of 1997. Gale was living in a halfway house in Chicago at the time and talked with Mom every week. My father had died a year and a half before. Mom had cared for him at home until the final two weeks when he had to be hospitalized. Dad no longer recognized her. He hadn't recognized the woman he adored for months. Doctors urged my mother to agree to let tubes be inserted down my father's nose and throat to keep him alive. Once again, my mother said no to doctors who thought they knew best. She told them she was taking her husband home to die in peace.

Months of caring for Dad had sapped vitality from Mom, as had the death of her sister, Marjorie. When I came home for that last visit, I took Mom's little poodle for a walk on Saturday morning. I noticed, on reentering the house, how stuffy it was, how dim and crowded with junk. After they retired, Mom and Dad used to go to garage sales, but the useless bric-a-brac they bought was collecting dust. The house badly needed repairs. The bathroom tub was unusable because it leaked too much. The night before, some plaster from the living room ceiling had fallen onto the weary shag carpet. I'd headed for the closet to get the vacuum cleaner. "Don't bother, honey," Mom said absently. "I'll vacuum later."

Neither my sisters nor I had any idea how ill our mother was until she called Lenore one night to ask her to drive her to the hospital. I have never seen my mother's death certificate, so I do not know what was listed as the cause of her death. I only know that when she checked herself into St. Joseph's, her heart had taken all of the loss it could bear. A month earlier, my mother had received a call from St. Francis Hospital in Evanston. Over the telephone, she repeated to me in a strangely calm voice—*hollow*, I think now—what hospital staff told her: Gale had been hit by a car that had left the scene. She had suffered multiple injuries and was in intensive care. I don't want to imagine what my mother went through that night, alone in a house where a family had once laughed and argued and shared meals.

I hesitated over mentioning the letters Gale sent to me after what I thought was a happy phone conversation about past Easters, but her accusations against "Helen" and "Arthur" were so ugly, I decided I had to. I told Gale how disappointed I was that she would send me such lies about Mom and Dad.

"You don't know what Helen was like back then!" she said almost petulantly. "You have no idea what I went through as a child. Let's just not talk about it."

I let it go. She was my sister, and I wanted to stay close with her. Gale went on to tell me about a "job interview" coming up, something to do with teaching arts and crafts to gifted children. Which meant, given her penchant for exaggeration, that she probably simply saw an ad in the paper. "I'm *perfect* for the job. I just hope the woman I talk with doesn't think I'm overqualified. Frankly, I think she'll be a little intimidated by my resume. Oh! I almost forgot to tell you: I wrote a new play! It's brilliant. It's got Jesus and Socrates and Satan in it, and it's hilarious! I'm sending you a copy tomorrow. And I'm sending one to a production company on the West Coast. I think there's a good chance they'll produce it."

Maybe one day I'll understand why the house where I spent so many happy years is always dark and unwelcoming in my dreams. And why the woman who has my mother's face is not at all like my mother, neither loving nor kind. Just once, I want to dream about my mother the way she was—the way she appears in a photograph I keep on my dresser. She's sitting in a backyard that is half sun and half shadow, looking straight at me and smiling. I took that picture of her one morning when Dad was still alive. It was the end of April, and we decided to drink our coffee out back. Her little dog was nosing through leaves. Mom showed me where a patch of violets was coming up. When I was a kid, they used to grow wild all over the neighborhood. Gale and I—it was always Gale and I—would go looking for them and bring home small, sweet bunches for Mom. Gale always knew where the thickest patches were. She knelt down in her red pedal pushers and picked each violet gently, never yanking or grabbing. Does Gale re-member this? Has she forgotten how Mom would exclaim over our bouquet and set a tiny vase of violets on the sill above the kitchen sink?

"Look, Frannie!" my mother said to me that half-sunny, half-shady morning I will never have back again. "They're almost ready to bloom."

Gale, curtseying to the camera at four years old.

THE BEST CHRISTMAS

Russell Wonderlick lived across the street from us. He was the only person in the world who called my dad "Artie," a nickname that irked my father, and he was always asking if he could "borrow" our *Joliet Herald* "once you're done with it, folks, not a minute before!" Still, when I was in fourth grade, Mr. Wonderlick gave our family a wonderful present: a glittering white bell that played "Silent Night" when you pulled down its tongue.

My father made it his mission to keep me and my sisters from constantly doing just that. "This bell is not a toy! It will last for ten years, it will last for a *hundred* years, if you treat it properly." Claire and I did not treat the bell properly. It was far too enjoyable to grab the string and yank. In a matter of days, exactly as my father had predicted, the marvelous bell was broken, its long tongue lolling from the kitchen doorway where Mom had hung it. That was the only bad thing I remember about the Christmas of 1967.

Part of the reason it was such a good Christmas was the guilt my mother felt over the previous one. Mom never *said* she felt guilty, but I realize now that she must have. The year before, we'd gotten our presents early. Dad took us for a ride after supper to see the decorated houses of Joliet. This was not at all like my father, but Mom was adamant about how enjoyable it would be for me and Claire. Maybe my four older sisters had to crowd into the station wagon as well. When we got home, I was informed gaily by my mother that Santa had paid an early visit. At eight years old, I no longer believed in Santa Claus, but that was the way my mother put it. My presents were grouped on the dining room table. They included a metal dollhouse—nothing like the dollhouse at Steinberg-Baum that had real furniture and tiny lamps that really lit up—and a pair of mittens.

It had been a hard year, financially, for my parents. Their piano store was barely staying afloat. That was the year that Dad started working at the Uniroyal tire factory and Mom started managing the store. My mother must have been exhausted that Christmas Eve. This did not occur to me. I was crushed that I wouldn't get to wake up in the middle of the night, race downstairs with my sisters, and find out what surprises awaited. We'd *always* done this. After tearing into our presents, we had hot chocolate in mugs shaped like elves' heads before going back to bed. I tried not to act disappointed, but my mother must have known I was. She made up for it the following year.

Christmas season began by going up to the attic with Mom and helping her bring down boxes of decorations. When they were stacked in the dining room, Claire and I got to unwrap them, leaving drifts of yellowing newspaper on the floor.

"Look! This box has the Crib."

"I bet this is Jesus," Claire said, snatching a small, square chunk.

"Give it to me! I had it first!"

We dug into the box, ripping newspaper away from plaster of Paris shepherds and lambs. Mom let us set up the Crib ourselves, which meant that we were soon arguing over where to put Joseph and Mary and what to do with the plastic goat, twice as large as the lambs, that had somehow become part of our Nativity set. Claire was unsentimental about him.

"He doesn't belong. Let's throw him away."

But the goat—laughable to me just a minute ago—suddenly seemed to be looking at me with sweet and utterly defenseless eyes. "We can't throw him away!"

"He's only a piece of *plastic*." We compromised by hiding the goat behind the stable. When Claire wasn't looking, I poked his face through the window so he wouldn't feel entirely left out.

It was important to me that every single room in our house be decorated, even the bathroom. My mother obliged, draping a garland of fake holly across the top of the medicine cabinet. Dad wrapped the two front porch pillars with red plastic ribbon so they looked like giant candy canes. We decorated the tree with cheap ornaments I considered priceless. I got to hang the Wiseman with the blue turban (the other two had rose and green turbans) on a branch of our fragrant tree. Our house was ready for Christmas.

Claire and I both wanted Madame Alexander dolls, and we knew exactly which ones. Claire wanted the dark-haired beauty representing Russia, and I wanted the golden-haired lovely who was Amy from *Little Women*. We had coveted these dolls for months, visiting them whenever we went to the toy department of the Boston Store downtown to make sure they were still there, that some stranger hadn't snatched them away from us. I knew that at my age, it was dangerously uncool to want a doll. I would never have admitted it to anyone at school. But Amy had real ringlets and a ruffled pinafore you could unsnap. She was irresistible. Anyway, Claire assured me, Amy and Tanya—Claire had already decided on the Russian doll's name—weren't like baby dolls. "These are *collector's items*, Frannie. That means we have to keep the boxes and be really careful when we play with them." I didn't care about Amy being a collector's item, but I was relieved to learn I had an excuse to still want, at the age of nine, a doll.

I was fairly sure I was getting Amy. Two presents exactly the size of Madame Alexander boxes, one for Claire and one for me, tantalized us from their place under the tree. Since no one believed in Santa anymore, Mom did things differently this year, slipping wrapped presents for the six of us girls under the tree when no one else was around. Claire and I spent part of every evening trying to guess who was getting what. We were especially curious about two unwieldy packages for us, about the same size as the doll boxes, but heavier. They obviously weren't board games or clothes. We knew we were too old for *toys*, so we couldn't imagine what was inside those packages.

St. Patrick's Grammar School was closed on Christmas Eve Day, which was sunny and sparkling. Mom went grocery shopping in the morning. Claire and I took advantage of her absence to play a game we'd invented: one of us lay on the dining room table while the other, after a running start, grabbed the feet of the sister who was lying down and *pushed* as hard as she could. She flew backwards almost to the other end of the table, to which we'd added the three leaves we used at suppertime. It was great fun until Claire pushed too hard and I flew off the table. I thought for a second, in mid-air, that I was going to sail right out the window behind me. Miraculously, when I landed, I was more shaken than hurt.

I wasn't mad at Claire; she would never push me off the table on purpose. Claire and I fought hard, but we were also best friends. When we were younger, we used to go on treasure hunts together, hoping to find some secret nook in our house that contained a surprise. Once, to my delight, I found just that: underneath our china cabinet lay a shining spread of nickels and dimes. "I found it! I found the treasure!" I screamed to Claire. I did not guess that my big sister, then perhaps eight, had put the stash there for me.

We didn't mention our game to Mom. I don't remember what she made us for lunch that day, but we were probably too excited to eat much of it. That afternoon, we brought carefully wrapped plates of sugar cookies to three elderly ladies who lived in our neighborhood, beginning with Mrs. Douglas, who lived on Hunter Avenue, and ending with Mrs. White, who lived on Willow. We rang their doorbells eagerly, knowing how pleased they would be to see us. The warm glow of virtue bathed us as we walked home.

Amy and Tanya were indeed waiting for us under our tree that year, along with two plump sewing baskets, pink for Claire and blue for me, filled with brand-new scissors and needles and a rainbow assortment of threads and material. Those were the two best presents, but we got plenty more. For once, my mother spoiled us. I was a little dazed by the wealth of gifts I received from my parents and relatives. I remember that Katherine received a substantial book filled with photographs entitled *Fifty*

Great Films, and Gale got a beautiful volume containing replicas of a hundred masterpieces of painting. I spent hours poring over those books, learning about films like *The Bicycle Thief* and studying, without realizing it, paintings by Rembrandt and Van Gogh. Those two volumes contributed as much to my education as any class I took at St. Patrick's.

Christmas Eve night, I took my first "grown up" bath using the Strawberries and Cream bubble bath that Katherine—now an Avon lady—gave me. Then I put on my new robe and slippers and went back downstairs to listen to the album of Big Band music we girls had bought for Dad. At our urging, Mom had changed into the hot pink lounge pajamas we'd presented her with. She claimed they were lovely. Myra and Gale jitterbugged to *Big Noise from Winnetka* and *Sing Sing Sing* while Dad collected wrapping paper to toss into the fireplace. "Through with that paper, Katherine? Hand it over. You too, Frannie. You girls bought me a fine present. Reminds me of going to dance halls in Chicago." But when I think about that Christmas, my walk home with Claire is what I like most to remember.

The afternoon glittered with just the right amount of snow and no wind. I knew the best was yet to come; our family would open presents after supper in front of a crackling fire. I would finally discover what that mysterious package contained, and whether my mother had listened to my pleas for a pant suit. Yet somehow the anticipation of all this made my heart so full I knew it could not get a chink fuller.

"Sometimes *before* you get something is even better than getting it," I said to Claire, whose cheeks were pink. Even with her horn-rimmed glasses, she looked pretty. This surprised me. I had never thought of Claire, who was the tallest girl in her class, and wore her hair pulled straight back in a ponytail, as pretty.

"You're right. It is."

"But why is that?"

Claire considered while I blew white clouds with my breath as hard as I could, something I would never do on the playground at school. "Well, like right now. We know what's going to happen tonight, but we've got this, too. So in a way, we've got *more*."

"Do you think we'll remember this day? Because you never know what you're going to remember."

"I know I'll remember it! I'll remember how you flew off the table." We burst into giggles.

"I'll remember—" I was going to say, *how good it feels to be with you right now*, but it seemed like a dumb thing to say. Claire could be unbearably bossy. Sometimes I hated her, but even when I was little—when Claire was still Dodo—I recognized something fine and brave about my older sister. She didn't care about being cool. She wasn't afraid to be herself. I didn't tell her that on our walk home. I knew that whatever happened, we'd always be best friends. I could tell her later.

Becoming a Writer: Eleven

Gordon Dilday hated Christine Hummel. A lot of boys in my sixth grade class picked on Christine. Girls did, too. But Gordon Dilday *hated* her. You could see it in his pale blue eyes. Gordon Dilday had shown no mercy to anyone since first grade. Three years ago, he knocked me off my bicycle when I rode past his house on Hunter Avenue. He laughed when I fell to the sidewalk, scraping my knees and cutting my chin.

Now I was eleven and Gordon Dilday sat across the aisle from me in Religion class. Our regular teacher, Mrs. Martis, couldn't teach Religion. She was what priests and nuns called a layperson. So every day after lunch—a time when the room stank, thanks to too many lunch boxes and too many sweaty kids who had just come in from recess—Father Pietree swept into our classroom in a black suit and starched white collar and taught us about Catholicism. Father Pietree, or Peach Tree, as the boys called him, was tall and big-shouldered, with a pink face and tiny eyes that didn't smile even though he clowned around a lot. He loved to joke with the popular boys, slapping them on the back and asking them about our chances for a basketball trophy this year.

We were studying the doctrine of Transubstantiation: how the bread and wine at the Last Supper became Jesus. I liked that word—*Transubstantiation.* It sounded deep red and golden to me, the way *Eucharist* sounded white and gold, and *Annunciation* blue and silver. But the doctrinal details of the Transubstantiation were boring. I kept a book inside my oversized text so I could read during class. Today I had brought a paperback called *The Family Nobody Wanted.* It was about a couple who adopted children of all races. My favorite part in the book was when five-year-old Rita, who was Mexican and had long eye lashes and shiny patent leather hair, proved to some stuffy old ladies from the adoption agency that she was every bit as pretty and smart as any blue-eyed blond little girl. I wanted to re-read that chapter, but I couldn't concentrate because of Gordon Dilday. He had written a note and stuck it on the back of Christine Hummel, who sat in the desk in front of me. The piece of notebook paper taped on the back of her green-plaid vest said in blue ball point: I AM A FAT PIG. But Gordon was not content with that.

"Hey, Hummel. I just put a note on your back, and I'm ordering you to keep it on. Don't take it off or else."

Gordon and another boy laughed. It sounded like they were snorting.

"Look, she's afraid—she's going to keep it on!"

"It says you're a pig, Hummel. How do you like that?"

Looking at the dark-green slope that was Christine's shoulders, it was hard to tell what she was thinking. It felt to me like she was trying to make herself smaller. Trying to disappear. Christine Hummel joined our class in fourth grade. She was a plump girl with pasty white skin and big brown eyes that looked scared. Kids knew she would be easy to tease right from the start. Boys called her names in the hall. Girls froze her out of games on the playground.

This year, when the bell rang at the end of recess and we lined up to go inside, the girl standing behind Christine was supposed to tap her shoulder, then turn to the girl behind her. "Hummel's germs, pass them on!" I never started Hummel's Germs, but sometimes I passed the germs on. I was too cowardly not to because I could get made fun of for having the germs. The last girl to pass Hummel's germs on to me was Jeannie Foley. She was laughing when she did it, as if she had no idea she was saying something that might be killing another girl in line. I felt a spasm of hatred for Jeannie Foley. For Gordon Dilday, too.

Gordon's buddy nudged him.

"Look at Tolf. She's all red."

"Better not take it off her, Tolf!"

"Shut up, Dilday."

"*You* shut up. Or I'll tell Peach Tree you're reading a book."

I was so full of fury at Gordon Dilday and hurt for Christine that my legs were trembling. I snatched the note off her back and crushed it into a ball.

"You'll be sorry, Tolf," Gordon hissed. His hand shot up.

"Yes, Gordon?" Father Pietree never noticed when kids tortured Christine, but he saw Gordon's arm right away.

"Tolf's reading a book, Father. It's inside her religion book."

"Really!"

Father Pietree strolled over to my desk. Everyone was watching; I could tell he was enjoying himself. "What are we reading, Francine?"

I felt myself turn even redder as I mumbled the title.

"The family . . . nobody . . . wanted." The way Father repeated what I said made students giggle. "Do you think a make-believe family is more important than the Transubstantiation, Francine?"

It's not make-believe! It's based on a true story. Why didn't you say anything to Gordon Dilday for tattling?

"No, Father."

"Of course you don't." Then he put on a sad face. "And you don't want to hurt my feelings, do you?" More giggles.

"No, Father."

He said in a different tone, "Then give me the paperback. You'll get it at the end of the day."

Normally, Father Pietree left after Religion class, but Mrs. Martis had a meeting, so he was teaching us Social Studies, too. We were studying Central America—exports, imports, natural resources. Father Pietree told us that today's class would not concern Central America. He had a surprise for us.

"Any of you guys ever heard of the *Hindenburg?*"

No one raised a hand.

"Anyone know what a dirigible is?"

Tim McGovern did. Tim was one of those boys Father Pietree usually ignored because he was good at science, not sports. "It's an airship—designed so you can steer it. A dirigible's like a blimp, only bigger." It occured to me that Tim McGovern probably knew what the *Hindenburg* was, too. But he was smart enough to know that Father Pietree wanted to be the one to tell us.

"Correct," Father responded crisply. "And in the 1930s, way before any of you were born, way before *I* was born, lots of folks thought dirigibles, not airplanes, were going to be the commonest form of air travel. The *Hindenburg* was the name of the most famous dirigible at the time."

Father Pietree was walking around the room with his hands clasped behind his back as he told us this. He acted like he was on stage. I didn't like him, but I was interested. He told us about the *Hindenburg's* voyage on May 6, 1937—how the crew attempted to moor it in a place called Lakehurst in New Jersey, but then something went terribly wrong. With sixty-one crew members and thirty-six passengers, it burst into flames in the sky. He had everyone's attention now. When he told us people were burned alive or jumped to their deaths, girls gasped and the boys were fascinated. I was, too, in a terrible way. I didn't want to picture what Father Pietree was describing, but I couldn't help it.

Back in front of the classroom, Father Pietree paused and looked up and down the rows of students. "I've brought a record of the actual event. A live broadcast by a reporter named Herb Morrison. It's a very famous broadcast. You're going to hear it now."

Bill Hennessey, who always helped with audio visual equipment, had wheeled the cart with the record player to front of the room and plugged it in. Father solemnly placed the record on top and lifted the needle to play it. We were perfectly still, waiting for the live broadcast.

At first, there was nothing but scratches. Then the reporter's voice, thinner and higher than I expected. He was talking very fast, but I could make out words, and it wasn't long before I heard, *"It's burst* into flames! It burst into flames, and it's falling, it's crashing!" Some of the boys in the back corner, the boys Father loved to pal around with, were starting to snicker. "It's crashing terrible! Oh, my! Get out of the way, please! It's burning and bursting into flames . . . Crashing, oh!"

The snickers grew louder. I didn't understand these boys. This reporter's voice was kind of odd, but I could hear his horror. I could see the people jumping to their death, and it was sick-making. When I heard, "Oh, the humanity!" I wanted to cry. The boys in the corner were not even trying to hide their laughter anymore. How could they think this was funny?

"Hey, guys, keep it down over there. This isn't a comedy." Father Pietree was trying to sound tough and in charge to the rest of us and at the same time let his basketball stars know he wasn't really mad. He had told us about the *Hindenburg* as if it were important and tragic, as if it mattered, but now he was acting like it was okay to laugh about it.

When school was finally over and I was walking down Willow Avenue with Adrienne Wakinski, I couldn't shake off the horror of that broadcast—"*Oh, the humanity!*" Why had Father Pietree made us listen to it? I knew the answer: he wanted to impress us. He wanted to show us he didn't need to follow Mrs. Martis's lesson plan. But I wasn't impressed, I was heartsick. I knew Adrienne wouldn't understand. Adrienne didn't seem to get passionately angry or upset about anything. Even though she wore goofy hats crocheted by her mother and giggled really loudly, she never got singled out by bullies or popular kids. *She* never got knocked off bicycles. Adrienne chattered about her painting lessons with Mr. Hathaway, a local artist. "I learned how to paint trees last Saturday," she told me cheerfully. "This Saturday, I'm going to learn how to do clouds." Normally, I was jealous when Adrienne told me about her progress in art. My parents couldn't afford private lessons. That day, I didn't care. I was thinking about what I wanted to do when I got home.

The house was empty when I unlocked the front door and stepped into the living room where my cat, Boots, was stretched across the piano bench. Claire, I remembered, had an early piano lesson and Mom was at the piano store. After dumping my book bag on the dining room table and grabbing some Fig Newtons, I walked into the sun room and sat down at the desk where my father prepared his piano tuning bills. Usually if I sat here it was to draw, but today I wanted to write. I took out a clean piece of notebook paper and chose a sharpened number two pencil. I wanted to write about how boys laughed when that reporter was crying and about Christine and Father Pietree and Gordon Dilday. And about what a coward I was. Sure, I ripped the note off of Christine's back, but I didn't say anything to her. I had never said one nice word to her.

But where to begin? In real life, everything was connected to something else that was connected to something else. I had never tried to write about real life before. To put even one hour down on paper seemed impossible. I didn't feel that way when I wrote poems. My mother loved my poetry. So did my teachers. I wrote poems about flowers and sunsets and how beautiful the world was. Last week, I wrote a poem called "Miracles." I knew it by heart:

> The world is full of miracles.
> You'll see them if you try.
> Just watch a rose uncurl at dawn
> or hear a baby's cry.
>
> The moon and stars are miracles
> and so are sunset skies,
> but not till we unlock our hearts
> and open up our eyes.

I liked "Miracles" when I finished it, but I didn't *need* to write it, the way I needed to write about what happened that day. I was determined not to get up before I got at least part of this day down on paper the way it really happened. It was important.

October sun slanted in rectangles across the desk. The cuckoo clock ticked loudly.

Doors slammed, sisters came home. Someone turned on the radio in the kitchen.

Katherine poked her head in the door and asked me if I would set the table. I said yes thankfully. And slipped the piece of notebook paper, which was still blank, back into the desk's middle drawer.

READING

. . . with a quick glance around to make certain that neither Aunt Sarah nor Uncle Matt would see her, she went inside. The little room was cool, sweet and fresh, and perfectly dark. Tom caught hold of her roughly, one arm about her waist, his hand immediately sliding down into her blouse as he sought for her lips. Obviously this was not new to either of them, and for a moment Amber submitted . . .

"Francine."

Curled deep in the big chair in our living room that blissful summer afternoon, luxuriating in the Joliet Public Library's one copy of *Forever Amber*, which I had finagled from Claire only by promising to do her share of the dishes that evening, I jumped. How long had my mother been standing behind me?

"Hi, Mom!" I tried to look as innocent as a twelve-year-old possibly could.

"You are too young to be reading that."

"But Mom—"

"No buts. I don't want to see you with that book."

I had to hand Mom the coveted library book whose musty fragrance and orange binding I still remember. And by doing so, promise I would not read it again. How could I keep that impossible promise? I couldn't. Furtively, and with deep delight, I devoured all 652 pages (and that with double columns) of *Forever Amber*, who went on to lose her virginity not to country bumpkin Tom but to muscular, green-eyed Bruce, a nobleman, and who eventually became the mistress of Charles II. It was the first time in my life I deliberately disobeyed my mother. Such was the power of author Kathleen Winsor that I did not even suffer much guilt.

Twelve was an odd age. I was as likely to settle down with *Class Ring*, in which a bubbly sixteen-year-old named Toby knitted argyle socks—whatever *they* were—for her boyfriend, as I was to pick up *No Exit* or *Tess of the d'Urbervilles*, college paperbacks from my sister Katherine's bedroom bookshelf. Gladys Malvern, whose beautiful heroines, whether indentured servants in New Amsterdam or aspiring actresses in Edwardian London, *never* lost their virginity, was a huge favorite that year, as was mystery writer Victoria Holt. (Ditto with her heroines, although they were plainer than Gladys's and alarmingly older: twenty-six, sometimes twenty-seven or twenty-eight! Aging governesses who nevertheless ended up marrying the cruel-lipped masters whose arrogance gave my stomach delicious butterflies).

Although I made regular trips to the downtown library, my best friend Patti and I frequented the bookmobile as well, which parked at the corner of Willow and Morgan every other Tuesday afternoon from 3:00 until 5:00. In the summer, searching rows of books that smelled comforting and old, like the library itself, we could hear tinny renditions of "Red Wing" from the ice cream truck parked just up the street. The bookmobile's driver always wore a pressed blue shirt and had a modest afro. All the neighborhood kids loved him even though he insisted on quizzing us before we stepped down from his small kingdom with our books.

"Young ladies, what state in this great country of ours is known for its potato crop?" Patti and I blushed and giggled through every answer. Maine? Ohio? "Ohio!" Mr. Bookmobile's eyebrows shot up in mock dismay. "Oh, man, them teachers of yours got a lot of work to do. A *lot* of work. I'll let you off this time, but you got to promise me you're going to read some *geography*."

I loved to read, but I read only fiction: *The Wind in the Willows*, *Rebecca of Sunnybrook Farm*, anything by Laura Ingalls Wilder or Louisa May Alcott. Happy as I was climbing garage roofs and playing frozen tag after supper, subtracting books from my childhood would be taking away a second world I loved almost as well, and sometimes more, than the one I lived in.

I could read before I entered the first grade at St. Patrick's Grade School—hardly surprising, since I had five older sisters and lived in a house where bookshelves overflowed. Plus I was read aloud to often, most memorably by Katherine, who wanted to be an actress and had a wonderfully expressive voice. Katherine brought alive the adventures of Winnie the Pooh and Dorothy in her travels throughout Oz. She also told Claire and me stories she made up herself about a flower kingdom inhabited by two rival fairies, May Bloom and June Blossom. At five, I firmly believed in such beings. I believed the two guardian angels framed above our twin dressers, one petting a lamb, the other picking roses, truly looked after Claire and me. I was convinced every stuffed animal I owned, even the most worn, would have been wounded if I did not hug it good night.

Around that time, I remember, my father gave Claire and me a pair of black frames that had held the lenses for his reading glasses. He said they were magic. My sister and I took turns putting on those frames, far too large for us, before we went to bed. We claimed to glimpse elves dancing under the streetlight on Willow Avenue. Sometimes Daddy would tell us bedtime stories about two hobos, Pete and Jake. Even at five, I sensed how he struggled with those stories. They weren't nearly as good as Katherine's, but I didn't care: *Daddy* was telling them.

Gale had no trouble at all inventing tales about beautiful gypsies and mermaids. She even illustrated them. And Myra always had us laughing when she described the misadventures of two witches named Elizabeth and Marie—our middle names. But when it was Lenore's turn to tuck us in, we were likely to face the dark scared. Lenore liked reading Claire and me Bible Stories. She picked out the scary ones, like when Saul visits the witch of En-dor, who conjures up the ghost of Samuel.

Worst of all was the night Lenore read us "The Royal Ram" from the *Golden Book of Fairy Tales*. In that story, Wonder, a beautiful young princess who befriends a prince who has been changed into a ram, leaves him to attend a family banquet. The lovesick prince finally can stand her absence no longer and runs to the palace gates, begging to be admitted.

> *. . . He was rudely refused. He dashed back and forth, distracted, afraid that he had lost his beautiful Wonder forever.*
>
> *He begged the guards to admit him. They laughed, and turned away. Finally, in a transport of grief, the ram lay down at the gates and died.*

When Claire and I heard that, we wailed. Our grief was loud and inconsolable. Mom came in to talk with us. I don't know what she eventually did or said to calm us down, but I'm guessing the next time Lenore read from the *Golden Book of Fairytales*, she chose a story that ended happily.

Little surprise that by September of my sixth year, I could read on my own. My first-grade teacher had no way of knowing this. She was a beautiful brown-eyed nun by the name of Sister Christina Mary, and for some inexplicable reason I was terrified of her. I was also terrified I would forget my homework, not know the answer if called on, and, most dreadful of all, be late for school. St. Patrick's was only a block and a half away, but every morning I left our house far ahead of my five older sisters. Mom used to sigh, she told me later, as she watched me bound like a frightened deer across the Quigley's yard, clutching my clear plastic book bag. I arrived at the school playground a full quarter of an hour before the bell rang.

It was weeks before I relaxed enough to walk to school with a fellow classmate, Adrienne Wakinski. Adrienne lived on Willow Avenue but was willing to come to my house (we lived on Raynor, one block west) then, with me in tow, double back to Willow. She was a stolid child with no tact.

"Mrs. Tolf, I'm in the smart reading group," she announced to my mother one morning as I was finishing my bowl of cream of wheat.

"Isn't that good for you, Adrienne," my mother replied in a light voice she used when she was trying not to sound annoyed. "What group is Francine in?"

Adrienne giggled. "She's in the dumb group. But it has a better name than ours." Then, turning to me. "*You* get to be a Cotton Candy. I like that better than being a Candy Cane."

"Me, too," I said, meaning it. I had not told Mama about my low ranking. Until Adrienne pointed it out, I thought Cotton Candy was the smart group. I wasn't troubled to find out it wasn't, but my mother was. She had a talk with Sister Christina Mary, explaining that although I could read perfectly well, I was very, very timid. Sister must have made a special effort to be nice to me, because some time that autumn my terror of her turned into infatuation. I moved into Candy Canes.

You had to be seven to get a library card at the Joliet Public Library. I went there a few days after my birthday, the summer of 1965, and was excited to receive the thick, round-edged card which had a little metal bar inserted under my typed name. Children's cards were orange and adult's were blue. If you had an orange card you were limited to books from the children's library, a wonderful room with deep window sills and a fireplace tiled with pictures of pilgrims and Indians. By the time she was ten, Claire, who read even more than I, would sometimes try to check out books that were not from the children's section. She would invariably be caught and chided by one of the ladies at the front desk. Or one might smile and playfully wag a finger at the tall, serious little girl with thick blond hair and glasses who wanted to check out *The Tudor Rose* or *The Nun's Story*. That infuriated Claire more.

She must have gotten Myra to check out the books she wanted. Myra sometimes accompanied Claire and me on our trips to the library. Trips anywhere with Myra were enjoyable. She'd invent games or have Claire and me laughing even if we *wanted* to be mad, for my third oldest sister was an incurable tease. Myra didn't like to read fiction the way Claire and I did. It always astonished me that she preferred reading about real people instead of imaginary ones. Claire and I would come home with fictional books by Maude Hart Lovelace and Frances Hodgson Burnett. We'd spread our bounty on the dining room table alongside Myra's choices: a plastic-bound biography of the Lennon Sisters (they sang regularly on Lawrence Welk), or *Yes, I Can!* by Sammy Davis, Jr.

Lenore never went to the library at all, as far as I can remember. But she did buy paperbacks about the life and readings of the late psychic Edgar Cayce. Lots of paperbacks. Lenore began claiming as a teenager to have had an out-of-body experience when she was six. She was lying on the couch, she said, as Mom fried bacon in the kitchen. Suddenly her body rose but could not pass through the ceiling even though she saw the Virgin Mary's face high above in the sky. This struck the rest of us as hilarious. "Could you smell the bacon when you were rising?" Lenore would insist she could, which only made us laugh harder.

Lenore also read movie magazines. There was no *People* or *Us* in the sixties, only thin, tawdry magazines run by a gossip queen by the name of Rona Barrett, a tiny woman with swirled blond hair whose grinning face was always peeping above the shoulder of some starlet in the grainy black and white photographs inside. The paper was cheap, and there were ads in the back pages for fanny padding and bras with the tips cut out. Every month Lenore bought new copies of Rona Barrett's *Hollywood* and Rona Barrett's *Extra* and would hunch over pictures of Robert Culp and David McCallum, popular TV stars. She always took a stash of those magazines with her when she went on trips in the summer with Aunt Margie. While my other sisters pressed their noses to the window to get their first view of the Rockies, Lenore was buried deep in an article about the break-up of Elizabeth Taylor and Richard Burton.

As I moved from childhood to adolescence, I remember a number of less than literary books that were household favorites: *Gone With the Wind, Calico Palace, The Vines of Yarrabee.* But none so beat up with rereading as Taylor Caldwell's *Testimony of Two Men,* a story about a brilliant and arrogant doctor, Jonathan, who tames sweet, wild Jenny. If you picked up our copy of that swollen paperback, the pages fell open naturally to chapter eighteen, in which Jenny is almost raped, and which includes the following immortal passage:

> *. . . Jonathan was upon her, seizing one arm. He used his other to grasp the neck of her nightgown and rip it down her body to her knees. Before she could move, his hands closed around her slender damp waist, and he had pulled her to him and was kissing her mouth in a rapturous storm of desire. She struggled frantically. She tried to kick him with her bare foot, and he laughed, and his fingers pressed themselves into the warm flesh of her body, and his mouth held hers, forcing her lips apart.*

Mom was fighting a losing battle if she thought any adolescent girl could resist such prose. Nor was Mom herself immune to the best-sellers my older sisters brought into our house. *The Godfather*, for example, had "Filth!" written in my mother's strong hand . . . on the very last page. The truth is that most of Mom's paperbacks from the Catholic Book Club had a coating of dust on them. My mother loved Chesterton and C.S. Lewis, but books with Bishop Sheen on the cover looked as if they had never been read. And I doubt if she ever spent much time with *Lives of the Saints*, two handsome volumes that sat in a small book-case in the living room. The binding actually cracked as I opened a volume one afternoon when I was in seventh grade. I was soon trying to find the goriest martyrdom. One woman was crucified on a wheel that rotated as she bled to death, a strategically placed bucket catching every drop of her holy blood. I ran into the kitchen to tell my mother. She was horrified such stuff was in her house.

I wonder now whatever happened to those two volumes that sat untouched throughout my high school and college years. They were probably in the living room when I came home to visit Mom and Dad after I moved to Chicago. They might well have been there the last time I was under that roof, a few weeks after Mom's funeral. Three of my sisters and I had agreed to meet to go through papers and photographs and take what miscellaneous items we wanted. My mother didn't have any-thing of real value. Inexpensive dishware and glasses covered the dining room table that day. Everywhere were knickknacks, pots and pans, decades-old *Prevention* magazines, grimy to the touch. It was a crowded house. Lenore's five children were there, along with Myra's three and Claire's three. The afternoon was one long treasure hunt for the kids: they raced through rooms bickering over who could keep what.

Marc, the man I live with, urged me to take perfectly good mixing bowls, a toaster that had never been used. I wasn't interested. I wasn't interested even in the stack of spiral notebooks that served as diaries throughout my college years. I noticed those fat notebooks piled on a shelf in the closet of the southwest bedroom as family members went through dressers and cabinets. Part of me thought, *these were precious to me once, I must not leave them here.* But that's exactly what I did. I felt a little sick from all the *stuff* everywhere, cluttering every room. Suddenly those pages and pages crammed with teenage angst and passion—written when I believed it was my destiny to become a writer—didn't seem precious at all. They just seemed like more junk. All I wanted was a photograph album that had pictures of Mom as a baby and a little girl. I looked everywhere, but couldn't find it. In the end, I took nothing.

I wish now that I had. I wish in particular I had taken some of the books I grew up with. By that time, many of them had been given away or appropriated by older sisters with families of their own. But there must have been some books from my childhood still up in the attic. Stacked on brick and board shelves, they must have been up there that day, untouched by human hands for decades, along with old board games and boxes of Christmas decorations. Maybe *Donna Parker Goes to Hollywood* or *Cherry Ames: Student Nurse*. Or maybe my illustrated edition of *Heidi*, the one I was given the winter I was eight and Claire was ten and received *The Five Little Peppers*. I remember sitting in front of the fireplace the afternoon we got those books and reading with Claire: the crackle of flames, the pungent scent of logs.

Claire remembers, too. When we were young women and still close, she told me that was one hour in her life that she was perfectly happy. We don't talk anymore, Claire and I. We had a falling out when I was in my mid-thirties. I said words that tore open a gap between us so wide I don't know if it can ever be mended.

But the contentment I felt reading next to her when I was eight is whole and flawless in my memory. My new book had a picture of Heidi dancing barefoot in a meadow of flowers. Claire's book had pictures, too. From a distance of over forty years, I watch two little girls turn their book's pages reverently, savoring every word. These are *chapter* books, so thick it seems it will take weeks to finish them. Claire and I know better. We don't want to reach the end too soon.

Frannie and Claire, circa 1969.

BECOMING A WRITER: TWELVE

Margie and Claire and I were riding the Hotel Monteleone's elevator down to the first floor. It was a very fancy elevator operated by an elderly black man wearing white gloves and a jacket with fringed epaulets. "Y'all have a pleasant evening now, Sir. Ladies, y'all have a lovely night," he gargled in a throaty voice as he slid open a grillwork gate, allowing guests to step out of mirrored doors.

We were not staying at the luxurious Monteleone, but we had just eaten at its fourth-floor restaurant for the second night in a row because the Creole seafood gumbo was so delicious. All three of us ordered it again, along with freshly baked loaves of bread and steaming bowls of fragrant rice. We were in New Orleans and it was two days before Easter, so in addition to being dazzled by the restaurant's thick white linen, shining silver, and cut glass, I was dazzled by the lavish displays of food and desserts it would serve for Easter Brunch.

I would remember those decadent culinary displays, banked against hills of lilies and hyacinths, unlike anything I had seen in Joliet. I would remember pink stucco walls and hidden fountains in the Garden District, riding a street car that really *was* named *Desire*, calling to sailors with Claire, who was fourteen, as the both of us leaned over our hotel room's balcony to view the river of tourists below.

"Hey sailor, this girl next to me thinks you're handsome!"

"Blow me a kiss, sailor!"

One boy, all of nineteen, looked up and *did* blow me a kiss. I was thrilled, but Margie was already hustling me inside the two-bedroom suite located in the heart of the French Quarter—quite an extravagance for my aunt. Usually on road trips, we stayed at Holiday Inns.

I would remember the tails of carriage horses in St. Louis Square braided with ribbons on Easter Sunday, fresh coffee and beignets at a riverfront cafe, barkers on Bourbon Street. At first, Margie refused to take us to Bourbon Street, but Claire and I wore her down with our begging. She finally agreed to *one quick walk* through the honky-tonk district "although I don't know why you girls want to see low-lifes, and I don't think your mother would approve. And do not look inside *any* of the bars!" We didn't need to; we heard about them as the three of us—a plump middle-aged lady in sensible shoes and two beanpole adolescents—walked past them. "Topless *and* bottomless, the most gorgeous girls you will ever see in your life!" I would remember those barkers with their muscular arms and their faces blue from neon.

But not as well as I thought I would. New Orleans would eventually recede into a handful of lushly colored but vague postcards. It was what happened in that fancy elevator of the Hotel Monteleone that mattered.

A man and a woman got on at the second floor. They were about Margie's age, but both were a head taller than her, distinguished and elegant. The woman wore a mink stole—*a real mink stole!* my eyes shouted to Claire—and what had to have been genuine diamonds in her ears and around her throat. I saw in the mirror how she seemed to bloom above my aunt, who was wearing a tan raincoat and glasses that made her look like an owl.

The woman in diamonds wasn't rude. Not exactly. She looked down at Margie, then looked away. But I knew—I didn't know how, but I knew—that the way she did that hurt my aunt. This stunned me. Margie had been a school teacher all of her adult life and was used to being in charge. She was bossy and generous and unfailingly sure of herself. But she wasn't as invulnerable as I thought. Actually, I had never thought about my Aunt Margie at all except for how she related to *me*. I had never considered her as a person in her own right, the way this woman with diamonds and beauty parlor hair was a person in her own right, with her own stories and her own secrets.

I felt something inside me opening with this understanding. My Aunt Marjorie, my mother and father, all the adults I knew had facets to their personalities that I might never learn about, fears and longings that had nothing to do with me. Maybe that was why my dad was hard on me, always saying, "You may be the youngest, but you're not the baby!" Maybe when he saw me, he saw his youngest brother, Elmer, who he said was spoiled. Maybe I was someone different to every person who knew me, and I would never know who they saw.

The world was at once clearer and a thousand times more complex than it was a few minutes ago. For some reason, I thought of a piece of glass I had when I was little—some kind of knob. I thought it was magic because it caught rainbows and cast them on walls and on the floor. I remember I was convinced that if I could only climb inside that piece of glass and look through it, I would see things as they really were. I felt as if I had finally climbed inside the glass, if only for a moment.

"Y'all have a wonderful evening now," the operator said as he opened the door to the hotel's gold and marble lobby. The elegant couple ignored him, but my aunt thanked him in her school-teacher's high, firm voice. Flanked by Margie on one side and Claire on the other, I stepped out of the elevator into a world I was not yet sure how to navigate. But I wanted to learn.

THE SUMMER BEFORE EIGHTH GRADE

I was at Inwood Pool on Jefferson Street, west of the fast food restaurants—Dog 'n' Suds, Franksville, Kentucky Fried Chicken—and used car franchises ("Bill Jacobs wants YOU to buy a Chevy!") that lined my hometown's main drag. It was the summer of 1971. I was twelve years old, wearing my first two-piece bathing suit. It was blue and white, with fake plastic zippers on the top and bottom. My body was hard and taut-bellied and tanned. I took no pride in it. But I liked my swimsuit, from which my belly button peeked out, because it had padding on top and made me look slightly less flat-chested than I was.

It was nearing 9:00 p.m., closing time, but the pool was still crowded. A group of teenaged girls, confident and flirtatious in their neon-colored bikinis, were laughing by its edge, combing their long hair, made blonder by Sun-In. Boys my age were roughhousing by the diving boards. I was not a good swimmer, but I could do what I called the breaststroke, paddling my legs and arms through the water like a frog. Sometimes I flipped over on my back and met a sky just beginning to deepen to lavender. Tall lights guarding the pool floated like white jewels at the edge of my vision. I dove underneath, where even Inwood's water, so full of chlorine your throat ached from it, held silence and mystery. I loved to resurface then, pop up from that netherworld of stillness and rippling shapes into splashing and happy screams. I liked being able to dip at will into one world, then the other.

I did my frog paddle across the pool one last time, gracefully as a mermaid, I was thinking, when it happened. Legs wide apart, I felt a hand grab my crotch, shove underneath my suit, and pinch me hard *there*, where no one had ever touched me. I snapped my legs shut, whirled around. No one. Or, rather, everyone. I made it to the side of the pool and clutched the ladder, looking at all the faces, all the bodies, around me in the water. *He's watching me. He's watching me right now, probably with his friends, and I'll never know who he is.* I wanted to cry, but I acted like nothing happened. I climbed out of the pool, feeling the film of his smirk on my skin. *He mustn't know he humiliated me.* I joined the two sisters I came with and started goofing around loudly, just in case he was still watching. I wanted what happened to me, the shock of it, every cell of my body crackling into an unscreamed *No!* when those fingers pushed their way into that private part between my legs, to melt away like the lavender melting into this soft black summer sky. I told no one what happened.

This was the summer I learned from my best friend, Patti, about oral sex. Patti got most of her sexual information from Karen Kirsten and TC Mc-Shane, girls two years older than we were who lived on Patti's block on Audrey Street. TC had light orange hair and pale blue eyes, as if they were washed too many times. Patti thought she was pretty, a genuine strawberry blond, but I thought TC looked a little spooky. Karen had long greasy hair and a languorous manner around boys. She wasn't popular, she wasn't even especially pretty, but she had her own lazy kind of confidence. Karen taught Patti an exercise that was supposed to make her breasts (or boobs, as Karen put it, a word I could never bring myself to use) bigger. Arms shoulder high, elbows bent, you repeatedly thrust your elbows back towards your spine as you recited: *We must! We must! We must develop our bust! The bigger the better, the tighter the sweater. The boys depend on us!* Sometimes, Patti and I did this exercise together, giggling hysterically.

It was Karen who told Patti about a book entitled *The Perfect O*. She made Patti guess again and again what the perfect O was. Finally, Karen told her. And Patti told *me* one Saturday night, when I was sleeping over at her house, as I often did. We were in her bedroom, where every available space was covered with pictures Patti had clipped from cards and magazines. There were puppies, kittens, angels, flowers, little girls whose sweet, chalky faces graced the packages of a certain brand of toilet paper, and four pictures that Patti had sent away for of the same thatched cottage in summer, fall, winter and spring.

We were changing into our nightgowns when my best friend disclosed her new knowledge. "They put their thing *in your mouth*. It feels so good for them, it's called the perfect oh. And the girl's mouth is round, like an O. So that's another reason it's called that." I couldn't believe it. I couldn't believe any girl would do such a thing. I wished Patti, who seemed more amused than disturbed, hadn't told me.

Actually, I had only a vague idea of what a boy's "thing" *was*. I had no brothers, only five older sisters. The few times I'd ever played with boys was when I was younger, when neighborhood kids got together to play Red Rover or frozen tag in the Quigleys' big yard next door to my house. I was too old for that now. I had never seen a boy naked. I knew they had to raise the toilet seat when they peed, but I was not exactly sure why. I would have died before asking anyone. The book that my mother left in my room for me one day was not very helpful about answering such questions. It was a Catholic book with tepidly drawn illustrations. I learned that masturbating, which was described quaintly as "pleasuring oneself," would not make me go blind, but that it was a selfish act, and wrong. I learned that I might soon begin menstruating. There were passages about eggs and sperm that bored me. I wanted to know what was between a boy's legs. No, I didn't. Whatever it was, was alien and scary. I didn't want to know.

――――――――――――――――――――

Patti and I had invented a game we called Chinese Torture. This game was different from the many others we had come up with involving ping pong balls, or acrobats, even an updated Barbie board game we made ourselves. We played Chinese Torture on Saturday night, when I slept over at her house. If it was my turn, I lay on the bed, while Patti ran her fingers as lightly as possible all over my body. We never touched parts that were covered by our nighties, only what was exposed. To succumb to a touch that delicate, the shadow of a tickle all over my skin, was crazy-making, but also enjoyable. We never went further than that. I loved Patti, but I loved her as a friend. Her body did not interest me. Yet I knew something was wrong about our game. It had to do with the crazy-making part, how that made the touch of my best friend *more* enjoyable. It was dirty, like the way I sometimes felt when I saw pictures of scantily clad women on album covers and in magazines. My older sister, Myra, had the sheet music to "You Only Live Twice." The picture on the cover showed James Bond sitting in a pool surrounded by seven or eight girls posed seductively in tiny bikinis. It attracted me, that picture; I wanted to be one of those girls just barely dressed, kneeling by James Bond. *No, I don't, I don't I don't. I want to be ten years old, playing frozen tag in the Quigleys' yard. That's what I want.*

———————————————

Sex had two sides to it, and adults only acknowledged the good side, the surface. That Catholic sex manual, for example, for all its lame illustrations, treated sex like a holy mystery. So did my mother. She took me aside one day after I blurted out something I didn't mean to, and explained to me gently but gravely that sex was a beautiful act that should only take place between two people who were married and loved each other. She dodged any specifics about the act itself, but she assured me of its beauty. What I learned from my friends about sex didn't sound beautiful at all. I thought of an afternoon last spring when I was walking home from school with Julie Baherling. Julie told me about a party where St. Raymond girls (we were St. Patrick girls) let eighth-grade members of their basketball team feel them up. "Then, they let them stick their hands down their pants. What sluts! The boys are just using them." Julie was fond of talking about girls who were just being used.

There was *that* part of sex, the stuff that really happened; there was the Holy Mystery part that I didn't get at all; and there was sex in books. *Katherine*, by Anya Seton, was currently my favorite book, and my favorite part of it was when John of Gaunt, Duke of Lancaster, kissed Katherine for the first time: *Fire shot through her, and as she gasped, her lips opened under his. In that instant she felt the hardness of his body under the velvet surcote and melting sweetness flowed through her bones, depriving her of strength.* Later, the duke carried Katherine away on his stallion to a castle where they made love in a tower room fragrant with reeds strewn on the stone floor. That was how it should be, I said to myself. Such descriptions turned my insides to water, but not in a dirty way. Not like the James Bond sheet music picture. I liked that phrase, "the hardness of his body under the velvet surcote." I wanted to feel a boy's body hard against mine.

One day that summer, not long after what happened to me at Inwood, I was chased by Patti's older brother and two of his friends. One of them was Toly Sandretto, tall, lanky, and very cute. It started out as a game in a wooded lot not far from Patti's house, something involving dares. Patti and I ran away together, but we got separated. I ended up cornered on the top steps of an old house where no one lived, the three of them, Mike and Toly and Andy, at the bottom of the porch, teasing and lunging for me. Without warning, the universe tilted. They were bigger than I was, these three boys. I saw nothing but taunting in their faces, which were blurring together. When Toly tried to grab me, I kicked out instinctively. I didn't make contact, but Toly backed away, startled. "Damn! What'd you do that for?" When I saw that he was genuinely alarmed, for his sake, or my sake, or both, the neighborhood tilted back, righted itself. It was just *them*. But my whole body was shaking.

I was deeply ashamed of my thoughts. If my mother, who I loved more than anyone in the world, knew I had them, I was sure she would be stunned and sorrowful. I felt more and more as if there were two sides to me: the bright surface and the netherworld. The brightness was what my teachers and family and friends saw. The netherworld was full of murky imaginings and dirty pictures that I must never, never disclose to anyone, not even the priest at Confession. I would rather have died with sin on my soul than have to describe these things. I prayed to God the Father, I prayed to Jesus, but it was Mary I felt closest to. Sometimes I went into St. Patrick's Church and knelt at the railing at the left of the altar where there was a statue of her, pure and white and tranquil. Not like me. I started checking things over and over before bedtime: whether the dresser drawers were shut just so, whether my pants were folded correctly. Sometimes when I was lying in bed, I got up and went downstairs to make sure all of the kitchen cabinet drawers were shut. Then, even after I had checked, I got out of bed again to make *really* sure. I was tired, but I did it. This was my way of punishing myself. But if I ever wanted to stop, I didn't think I could.

I read a lot that summer. I read *The Diary of Anne Frank*, finishing it one afternoon when I was by myself in the living room. I felt sick inside. I didn't understand why God didn't end the world before the Holocaust happened. I prayed hard to the Holy Spirit, that mysterious part of the Trinity that inspired no love in me, but supposedly gave courage to people. I prayed that, if tested, I'd be brave enough to hide Jews in my house. I didn't think I would be that brave, but I wanted to be, fiercely.

Another book I read was *The Bell Jar*, a paperback one of my sisters bought for a college literature class. Many of these college books were boring, like *The Human Ape* or *Tess of the d'Urbervilles*. But *The Bell Jar* was interesting and funny. Then, it turned dark. Esther talked about how she was never sure when the bell jar was going to come down on her again, how she had no control over it. I knew exactly what she meant. Sometimes pictures came into my head, and I couldn't get them out. Sometimes a kind of hopelessness mixed with dread came over me without warning. Then, it was like being under Esther's bell jar, unable to escape. It might last for an hour, or it might last for two days. No one else knew about this. All they saw was my bright side, my good side. I didn't know how to reconcile my surface with what was underneath. I contained two worlds, but it was not like the pool at Inwood where it was fun to dip from one into the other. I wanted to stay on the surface of myself, be the brightness everyone saw, but I couldn't, I kept slipping into the darker part.

Patti and I practiced our cartwheels and front handsprings almost every day. We made up cheers. Cheerleading tryouts were the first week of school, and we wanted badly to make the eighth-grade team. We were not popular, but maybe we would move into that elect circle if we were cheerleaders. My mother said nothing, but I knew she was disappointed that this meant so much to me. This was frustrating; why couldn't my mother be like other mothers who *wanted* their daughters to be popular? Yet a small, still part of me didn't want to be a cheerleader at all. It knew what made me happiest was being outside, and reading, and drawing. It knew that even though I talked with Patti about my crush on brown-eyed Mark Hayes (Patti had a crush on blue-eyed John Kinsler) I didn't really want anything to do with Mark physically. It felt, that part of me, like a small, true flame deep in my core, truer than the bad thoughts that came to me, steadier than the joyless moods that descended on me.

I lay in bed one night and thought about this. It was an immense relief to suspect that maybe the essence of me was not bad, but good. I would be thirteen in two weeks: a teenager. I wondered if I would feel different then. Confirmation didn't make me feel any different, even though the nuns and priests said it would. First Communion, so far in the distant past I could barely remember my little prayer book with the raised golden cross, didn't, either. But maybe becoming a teenager really did change you. Maybe this time, I would feel different.

My Dad, Finally

If you had met Arthur Tolf, you would have liked him. He had a firm handshake, a hearty "How're ya gettin along?" and a smile that lit up his Scandinavian blue eyes. My dad was a salesman, but his friendliness was no act. He greeted waitresses at Marishka's, where our family of eight had garlicky poorboy sandwiches, with the same enthusiasm he showed customers who walked into his piano store.

"A salesman sells *himself*," he'd say to me and my sisters. "And if you can sell yourself, you can sell anything! You girls can go into business for yourselves, not for somebody else."

The first thing Dad ever sold was rubber stamps. I know the story because it's one of the few my father enjoyed sharing about growing up in Joliet, the town where he was born, raised, and died. It was 1930, a year after the stock market crash. Dad was sixteen. Times were hard, but Alvar Tolf, a Swedish immigrant and gifted carpenter, was able to support his wife and his five children. Like many others, Dad's family had a pot of garden-grown vegetable soup simmering on the stove that they ate with day-old bread, but the Tolfs were not so bad off that Arthur had to drop out of school. I don't think any of his three brothers did, and I know that his younger sister, Evelyn, got her diploma. Arthur Tolf was restless. All his life, he admired people with education, but he was no book reader himself.

He left Joliet Township High, the limestone castle where I began high school forty-two years later, after his sophomore year. He'd been offered a full-time position as a stock boy at a downtown department store. The first day he was hired, the assistant manager ordered him to create a display of household items. Dad worked hard on his assignment. He never *said* this, but knowing my dad, I took it for granted. Whether it was folding towels, painting a closet, or attaching a bell to the handlebar of a bike, my father took pride in a job well done. As he was finishing up, the assistant manager surveyed Dad's handiwork.

"You call that a display?" the man demanded of the tall, blond kid he'd taken an instant dislike to. "You *happy* with that, Tolf?"

My father looked his new boss coolly in the eye. "Suits me," he said.

"I was fired that morning," my father would tell us, "but I got a job selling rubber stamps that same afternoon—and ended up *making more money!*"

Dad might have become a carpenter like his father and his oldest brother, Rueben. The signs he later painted for his own and other people's businesses showed an artist's sense of symmetry. For all I know, my grandfather, who died before I was born, might have *wanted* to teach his trade to his stubborn but smart boy. But from the way my father spoke about his father, it was clear that Dad believed otherwise. I grew up assuming my father was the son who always got the short end of the stick, the maverick who supported Franklin Delano Roosevelt in a house full of staunch Republicans. It wasn't until I was in my late thirties and had a few long phone conversations with my Aunt Evie, then retired and living in Arizona, that I was offered a different perspective. Evie insisted her father did not play favorites. Listening to her, one sees Arthur Tolf as a quick-tempered, sensitive young man who estranged *himself* from his family.

"After your father married, he almost never came by to see us. Ma used to sit on the couch and cry because she hardly knew her granddaughters!"

Evie believed this as firmly as my father believed that Elmer, his younger brother, was daily lavished with affection denied to him. Never

Dad's father, Alvar Tolf, with Lenore, Myra and Katherine, circa 1956.

mind that somewhere in between these emotion-charged memories lay the truth. My aunt and my father stuck to their own version of it—as we all do.

In any event, my father wanted a trade of his own. He found it in piano tuning. He was twenty-five when he enrolled in a course taught in Chicago by one Braid White. Even if I had never seen the photograph my father kept of his teacher, I'd have pictured him as he is in the photo: a tall man with a slightly stooped back, snowy hair, and a grave, kindly face. Braid White was one of those men who replaced, for Dad, the father he was convinced he never had. White wrote a number of well-received books on the art of piano tuning and occasionally published scholarly articles in journals like *Shakespeare Quarterly*.

He also, like my father, had perfect pitch. That, no doubt, was one of the reasons why Dad was able to teach himself how to play the piano when he was a kid. He had wanted piano lessons badly, but those went to Evelyn, his sister. Evie sometimes played hymns on her old upright piano when we went over to her house—the house in which Dad grew up—for a holiday. She played as one would expect a devout Baptist lady, who had practiced dutifully as a child, to play. Dad played like a maestro. His repertoire was limited to a dozen or so tunes—"Red Wing," "Hawaiian Wedding Song," "Ain't She Sweet"—along with snatches of classical music. But the way he caressed the keys and pedals of any piano he ever touched made for melodies that were rich and sweet and lingered in the air after he stopped playing.

Arthur Tolf was the only one of Alvar's sons to serve in World War II. Rueben, Albert and Elmer all got medical deferments. I remember those deferments coming up once or twice in conversations as I was growing up. I've forgotten what they were for, but I can't help thinking it terribly odd that out of four brothers, three were excused from serving in the armed forces. After Pearl Harbor was attacked, my father enlisted immediately.

The day he left for boot camp, Dad was driven to Joliet's Union Station not by Alvar, my grandfather, but by my great uncle Eston. When I try to remember Eston, his physical appearance blends in a dreamlike way with that of Braid White: my great uncle, too, was a tall, gentle-mannered man with a steady gaze that quietly assured you of his goodness. Neither Arthur, twenty-six, nor Eston, then in his fifties, would have been demonstrative as they drove from Garnsy Avenue on the East Side to the downtown train station.

"You take care of yourself, now," Eston might have said, keeping his eyes on the road. "Write your mother every week."

"Yes, sir." Dad loved Eston like a father. He seldom reminisced about his childhood the way Mom did, but those rare times he did, his uncle's kindness underlay every memory. "Eston used to buy me pineapple sundaes at the Sweet Shop . . . . wouldn't you like to try chocolate or butterscotch, he'd say, but I always wanted pineapple. He'd give me a dime so I could spend all Saturday afternoon at the Rialto. They had live acts in between the movies, but I didn't care about them or the movies as much as the man playing on that Grand Barton pipe organ."

Alvar could not understand why his son insisted on taking his brand-new set of tuning tools with him to boot camp. Maybe Dad didn't either, but he had those tools with him, wrapped carefully in felt and housed in soft leather, when he boarded a camouflaged train in the middle of the night and started to head west. "We knew what that meant," Dad said. "Headed east, you were going to fight in Europe. Headed west, you were going to fight in the Philippines. I wished we were heading East."

As it turned out, he fought on neither the Eastern nor the Western Front. Dad's unit had a several-day stopover in Hawaii. Through a coincidence I wouldn't believe in fiction, the U.S. Army's entertainment branch stationed there had need of a piano tuner for that night's performance of a play. My father offered his services. He ended up staying in Hawaii for three and a half years, working for the Entertainment Corps.

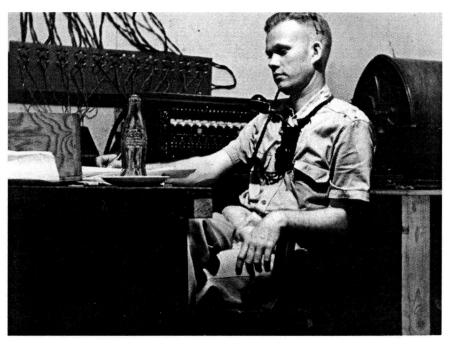

Private Tolf, June 1945.

Or, as my father put it, for "theayter people": grown men who pored over *Variety* in the morning before picking up a newspaper to read about the war. My father didn't despise *all* actors, but he didn't have a high opinion of very many. "Phonies," he called them. According to Arthur Tolf, there were few things worse than being a phony. You could be *goofy*—Dad's word for eccentric individuals. But you could not be phony.

Tall and slim, with golden-blond hair and bright blue eyes, Private Tolf kept to himself. Every day he read from a small, leather-bound New Testament that my mother gave me after Dad died. Perhaps it was a parting gift from his father, for both Alvar's and Arthur's names are inside, Alvar's script careful as a child's, my father's emphatic. He kept his barracks space immaculate and did laundry weekly, unlike other men who used the same towel over and over until, as Dad put it, "there was maybe a tiny, *tiny* clean spot on it, and they'd turn that dirty towel around and around until they found it."

Dad had one friend, though: a laconic man by the name of Tosheo. Tosheo ran a barbershop. Private Tolf spent his free afternoons there and sometimes had dinner with Tosheo's family. If certain soldiers didn't approve of an enlisted man being pals with a "Jap," it suited Arthur Tolf just fine. Again and again as we grew up, Dad told us to think for ourselves. "When I met your mother, I said to myself, 'That's the girl I'm going to marry.' Did I ask anyone if I was making the right decision? No! If you have to ask, then the answer is no."

Despite his dislike for the "phonies" he worked with, Dad said those three and a half years he spent in Hawaii were some of the best in his life. He ate fresh pineapple and took naps under palm trees. "I never seen a sun sink the way it did there. One minute the sky's full of color, the next minute the sun dips into the sea and it's night." Dad even managed to print up business cards and carry on a profitable tuning business on the side. This infuriated his corporal, who made numerous attempts to have him reprimanded. Dad might have been a corporal himself, but turned down the several promotions he was offered. He liked being a private.

"You know the first lesson I learned in the Army? *Don't volunteer for anything.* There were a coupla Italians (*Eyetalians*) in our outfit. Good guys. 'Tolf, they said, you know what you do when that corporal starts giving you the business? Act confused. Lift up one shoulder like this.'" And Dad would imitate the exaggerated shrug they showed him, head to one side, palms turned upward. Then he'd start to laugh. My father could never finish a funny story. He'd laugh so hard he couldn't talk anymore, so hard he would cry.

***

I was seventeen. My dad and I knelt beside the fire hydrant in front of our house, painting it red, white, and blue in celebration of the Centennial. It was a chilly day in early April. Cans of paint and rags and brushes cluttered the sidewalk.

"Don't get too much on your brush or it'll drip. *It'll drip! See? What did I tell you?*" The ragged, high-pitched irritation in my father's voice clenched my stomach into a familiar knot. He said in a different voice: "That's better. Now you're getting it."

If I were a different kind of teenager, I would have cracked a joke to ease the tension, but I couldn't. Instead, because I couldn't think of anything else to say, I muttered, "I'll try not to get too much paint on my brush."

My father was trying hard to be nice. I was trying hard to be enthusiastic. I wondered if he was as uncomfortable as I was.

This was all Mom's idea. Like painting a stupid fire hydrant was going to make us bond. My father didn't like me. I'd known this for a long time. It didn't bother me. I had Mom. I didn't need him. I didn't need this "togetherness." I was as nervous around him this afternoon as I used to be when I was little and found myself in the same room as he was, just the two of us. I never knew what to say. I still didn't.

"You got a nice smooth touch there, Frannie."

"Thanks, Dad."

A long time ago, he liked me. He threw me up in the air and called me Wickey Woo. He'd say:

Wickey Woo,

I love you,

Yes I do!

I was little more than a baby, so how could I remember this? Yet I did. The sky was blue, and green branches came close to my face, then flew away. We were both happy and laughing. Now my father criticized my hair and my clothes every morning before I was halfway down the kitchen stairs. He was always saying there was no such thing as an uncontrollable temper, but he didn't control *his* temper.

Last winter, I used the wrong utensil to adjust a burning log in our fireplace. My father went berserk. *Not that one! Not that one!* He was so furious, I ran into the cold without a hat or gloves and walked for blocks until the sun was an orange ball and I heard the cathedral bells telling me it was four o' clock. When I came home, half-frozen, he ignored me. My father didn't believe in apologizing. That was okay. I had my own protection now. When he was screaming at me or saying how dirty my jeans were, I repeated to myself, *He doesn't exist. He's not part of my reality.*

My father stood, stretched. I could tell his knees were starting to ache. "When we're done, I'll show you how to clean the brushes." He cleaned those brushes meticulously, I knew, and stored them in Hills Brothers coffee cans in his basement workroom, the room where he made each of us girls signs for our birthday that Mom hung in the kitchen.

"Okay. I know that's important."

"I don't know why he's so hard on you," Claire said to me: a huge admission from the sister who thought her father was perfect. Instead of telling her I was grateful that somebody finally acknowledged it, I acted indifferent. "How would *you* know?" I said, turning away.

It wasn't her fault that Claire got along with Dad, that of all my sisters, she was the one Dad felt special about. "A Swede like her father," Mom said about Claire. Claire loved pickled herring and strong beer and that pale yellow cheese Dad bought at Christmas, the kind that had caraway seeds. She was serious about the piano and believed, like Dad, that Martin Luther was a hero. I tried to tell Claire that Martin Luther may have reformed the Church, but he also believed in burning witches. She didn't want to hear about that. In Claire's book, as in my father's, people were either good or bad.

Maybe that's why they got along so well. In the shoeboxes of photographs no one had ever bothered to paste into albums, there were pictures of Claire wearing a pocket watch Dad gave her. She threaded a black shoelace through the handle and wore it around her neck when she was little. Claire was always sitting next to Dad in these old snapshots; she *liked* spending time with him. But I loved Daddy—I called him Daddy back then—too. He used to tell us bedtime stories about two hobos, Pete and Jake. I knew making up stories was hard for my father. I loved him for trying.

That was a long time ago. Now he hated me. Well, I hated him. "There are no favorites in this house," Mom was always saying. Yeah, right.

"I think we did a pretty good job. What do you think, Frannie?"

"It looks great, Dad. You did it, not me."

"I couldn't have done it without you. We're partners." He put his arm around my shoulder and squeezed hard, so hard my face crushed into his windbreaker. My dad, with his big hands and thick neck, the neck of a man, not a boy. I swallowed violently to get rid of the lump in my throat. *You are not going to cry, Godammit.* My father hated it when I cried. "Cut out those tears!" he said, as if tears were something you had control over.

Mom took a picture of Dad and me standing beside our patriotic fire hydrant. We smiled wide in the photograph, a father and his youngest daughter with paint brushes in their hands. A sunny spring afternoon. 1976.

My father died in 1995. I was thirty-seven. For years after his death, hurt and anger I never confronted him with when he was alive churned alongside love. The storm's over. I'm left with memories of a remarkable man I wish I had known better.

He had a modest dream: to own and operate a successful piano store in his hometown. And he did, for nearly fifteen years—first on Bluff Street, which overlooked the canal, then on Van Buren Street in downtown Joliet, across from Montgomery Ward and Barrett's Hardware. Dad stopped working full time at the piano store when I was in second grade and got a job at Uniroyal, a tire factory. I don't know if he made this decision on his own, or if Mom had to ask him, but I know that we needed the paycheck.

He started out driving a garbage truck, a job he claimed he liked just fine ("It's the best job in the plant!") because the bosses left you alone. Later, he became a painter. Dad made a few good friends at Uniroyal, but I don't think he cared for most of the men he worked with—men like Mr. Baherling, who lived up the street and also worked

My father, tuning our piano in May of 1965 . . .

at Uniroyal. Mr. Baherling strutted around his yard in an undershirt with a pack of Marlboros stuck under the sleeve. I remember my father once telling my mother about some "prank" that Mr. Baherling and some other boys at the plant had pulled. He sounded disgusted.

All this time, Dad never stopped tuning pianos evenings and on weekends. I think that he did this as much for social as for monetary reasons. He loved to tell Mom about the homes he visited—the mothers who served him cups of coffee and shared little details about their days, the children who watched him doctor their piano with his strange instruments, then were treated to "Happy Birthday" and "Jingle Bells." He had a soft spot in his heart for any family who owned a piano, for that meant they understood the importance of music.

And music, to my father, was bread. "Art Tolf Sells Happiness!" is what his hand-painted signs claimed. He kept a stack of those signs (black and red, accented with musical notes) in his pickup truck. If he noticed an opportune tree on which to advertise along one of the highways that led into and out of our town, he'd pull over and tack up a

. . . and tuning a piano at a school, circa 1976.

sign. It was against the law, but if a state patrolman stopped, Art Tolf, broker in happiness, talked himself out of a ticket.

Despite Dad's urging us girls to get into business for ourselves, he wasn't a good businessman. "Your father was a superb salesman," Mom told me once, "but it's lucky he had me to help him bid for franchises. Otherwise, he would have put in bids so low it would have been impossible to make a profit." I know that Margie bailed us out of near bankruptcy at least once. It had to have been hard for my father to accept the money, but he had already borrowed all he could from banks and spent the money representing his share of the family house where Evie, his sister, still lived.

Dad wasn't good at bill collecting, either. He wrote his own tuning bills in blunt yet graceful printing—all capital letters—and sent them out in hand-printed envelopes. Catholic schools were always slowest in paying. This incensed my father, but let Father Ryan from St. Patrick's, or Father John from St. Paul's, sincerely apologize for the delay and Art Tolf was soon insisting it was no trouble at all. "Take your time, Father, take your time! These days, it's rough for all of us."

With a wife and six daughters to support, and as the owner of a small piano store competing against larger, better financed ones, my father had his share of worries, but he kept them to himself. He was determinedly, sometimes *pugnaciously*, cheerful. He'd imitate the way Katherine, my older sister who wanted to be an actress, rolled her eyes when he talked about "theayter people." "What's on the ceiling there, Katherine? What are you straining your eyes for?" When I was a teenager, he'd needle me gleefully for what *I* considered a quiet mood and *he* saw as grouchiness. "Isn't it a great day to be alive, Frannie? Yes sir, a great day! A day to get things done *by the numbers*, like in the army! One-hup, two-hup, three-hup, come on, Frannie, say it with me!"

In 1970, when I was twelve, my parents bought a Yamaha Grand, a piano my father had always dreamed of owning. Even wholesale, it was a lot of money, but Mom never regretted their decision. When her Arthur played that Yamaha, she could feel his troubles melt into the music.

I was with my mother on the night my dad played that grand piano for the last time. I'd taken the train home from Chicago to spend the weekend. Dad had been near bedridden for weeks. That evening as Mom and I drank a glass of wine in the living room, he appeared at the top of the landing wearing only his underwear, looking solemn and a little unsteady. I don't think he knew who we were. He came down the stairs slowly, gripping the railing, then eased himself onto the piano bench. Mom and I didn't say a word. My father began to play. Melody after flawless melody rolled over the keys. When he finished, my mother and I burst into applause. My father stood up and looked at us gravely. Then, with dignity, he made his way back upstairs—stairs he would never again be able to navigate.

I don't know when my father stopped recognizing the people around him. My mother always insisted he knew her even when it was obvious he did not. There are some things we cannot bear to say out loud. My father said such a thing to me as he drove me to the Joliet train station one morning after one of my visits. This was well before the days that he was bedridden, when he would look at my mother and tell her he wanted the nice nurse. We were at the corner of Raynor and Jefferson, waiting for the light to turn green so Dad could make a right towards downtown. The light changed; my father looked around in a kind of panic.

"Which way? Where are we going?"

"Turn right, Dad," I said as gently as I could. "You're taking me to the train station, remember?"

My father looked down at the steering wheel he was gripping. I think if he had been alone, he would have covered his face with his hands and sat at that familiar corner for a long, long time. "I can't re-member things sometimes," he said softly, more to himself than to me.

I think of that moment now and want to reach down the years and hold him and promise him everything will be all right. What did I do that morning? I don't remember. He probably gave me one of his swift bear hugs before I got out of the car. He might have reminded me, a woman in her mid-thirties, to watch for sales at Jewel Grocery and avoid alleys at night.

"I will, Dad. I promise."

My dad, who fed the birds every winter and stood at the kitchen window watching sparrows and finches feast on suet he'd bought. Who cried when he read Luke 23:45: *Today you will be with me in paradise.* "Jesus didn't say tomorrow. He said *today!*" Who buried my cat, Boots, in our backyard and put a white stone over her grave.

My dad, who at one time I thought I needed to forgive.

My mother and father, circa 1980.

�֍Part Two✸

Fallout

The Tolf girls, Christmas, 1981. From left: Claire, Francine, Myra, Gale, Lenore, Katherine.

THE FIRST FUNERAL

About a year and a half before my father died, my parents stopped attending Mass at St. Patrick's, the parish where they'd been members for over forty years. Dad said it was because he was tired of going to church with "rich people"; he wanted to worship with "genuine people, people who aren't worried about what hats and shoes they're wearing in front of God." I learned later that a priest at St. Pat's had noticed Dad listening to a baseball game on his transistor radio while he ushered at Mass one Sunday. The priest talked to Dad about it. He may have been kind or he may have handled it badly, but Dad—who refused to admit he was wrong—never stepped inside St. Patrick's again.

His behavior was becoming more and more erratic. One weekend when I visited, Dad sat at the kitchen table as Mom prepared dinner. He began talking about Elmer, his youngest brother. "That Elmer, he was mean. A *selfish* brother. He never did anything nice for me, that Elmer." My father's lower lip was pushed out like a small boy's.

Mom took a pan of baked chicken out of the oven and turned towards her husband. "That's not true, Arthur," she said sharply. "When we first married, Elmer was a good friend to us. You shouldn't talk about him that way." Dad bowed his head like a chastened child.

That's the only time in my life I ever heard my mother use that tone with my father. I realized that her rebuke was a measure of the worry she lived with daily. *What am I going to do if Arthur gets worse? How will I take care of him?*

After Dad could no longer drive, Mom—who had not driven in twenty years—took him grocery shopping with her. But one afternoon at the Jewel, Dad got up from the bench where Mom had instructed him to wait and wandered out of the store. A woman found him in the parking lot. She asked him who he was looking for and brought him inside. Mom heard on the store's loudspeaker that an elderly man in a tan jacket was waiting to be taken home. After that, she did not leave the house for long. Margie or Ginny came over when she did her errands. They sat in the bedroom with Dad, who was too weak and too arthritic to walk much anymore.

I helped change my father one Saturday morning after having taken the train to Joliet the night before. Dad was a big man, six feet two, and his body was bloated. He was a dead weight to turn over, let alone lift, but Mom displayed amazing strength. At seventy-six, she handled him better than I did. Dad kept asking for the nice nurse; he told my mother he didn't like *her*. After we washed and changed him, Mom wiped each of his fingers with a warm wash cloth. Clean and dry, my father sighed like a child.

"Thank you, ladies," he murmured, sinking back into the bed. "Thank you very much." We gathered the dirty sheets and underwear. I followed Mom down to the basement to the washing machine and dryer. My mother looked so tired.

"Let me soak these, Mom, I'll put them in the wash later."

Mom opened the top drawer of the washing machine. "Just put them in the way they are, honey," she said. I understood then that what we were doing was a daily chore. My mother did not have the time to soak every sheet and diaper.

My mother took care of my father at home as long as she could. In April of 1995, with the help of Lenore and her husband, Bill, she brought him to St. Joseph's Hospital. I don't know if a particular incident prompted this decision, but I do know that twice, before she decided to hospitalize him, Bill had to come over in the middle of the night to carry Dad back up the stairs and into his bed. I also know that the first night my father spent at St. Joseph's was the first in many months that my mother slept through without interruption.

It may seem odd that I never asked about the specifics of my father's illness, yet I never felt the need to. I knew that Dad suffered from high blood pressure and severe arthritis in his knees. The past twelve months or so, his body had grown more and more bloated as his sense of balance decreased; if he stood up, he swayed like a great tree about to fall. He spent most of his time resting in the armchair in the dining room before even that became difficult and he remained in bed.

My father was in the hospital for only two weeks before Mom took him home. Doctors wanted him to stay; they wanted Mom's consent to put a feeding tube down his throat since he was too weak to eat. My mother refused. She knew her Arthur was dying, and she wanted him to die in his own home.

Bill set up a rented hospital bed in the dining room. My mother sat beside the bed for most of her day, reading and talking quietly to Dad. She slept downstairs, too. Lenore, Myra, Claire, and I all visited, and Margie and Ginny must have relieved her, but I think my mother needed this time alone with her husband. She was awake and holding Dad's hand when he passed away peacefully on a beautiful morning in May of 1995. Lenore called to tell me. After I hung up with her, I went to the bedroom and sat down on my bed. "I'm sorry we never knew each other better, Dad," I whispered out loud. "I know you loved me. I loved you, too."

Marc and I, who had lived together for five years now—a fact I did not allude to when visiting Joliet—rented a car for the funeral. We drove down to Joliet with Gale, who was then living in a group house at the north edge of Chicago. The funeral Mass was held at a church located on West McDonough Street. No one in the family except Mom had ever been inside it. It was the church my parents began attending after Dad refused to step foot inside St. Patrick's. The interior was modern and rather sterile, with none of St. Patrick's stained glass and statues. The woman who sang the hymns Mom had chosen was not very good—in fact, Dad would probably have hated her thin, reedy voice—but Mom later insisted what a lovely service it was.

Fewer people attended the Mass than had been at the wake, held earlier that morning; still, I saw a number of aging neighbors, including a frailer, slighter version of Mrs. Quigley. Claire, holding the hands of her two little girls, looked even more broken by grief than she had at the funeral home. She had obviously been crying the entire night.

After the service, when people were at the house, I wandered into the southeast bedroom Claire and I shared as children. When we went to bed, I remembered, we'd take turns putting on a pair of Dad's old glasses, pretending they allowed us to see elves glimmering beneath a street light on Willow Avenue. Today, Claire was standing by the dresser. "I know how hard this must be for you, Claire," I said, trying to sound as gentle as I could. "You and Dad were so close."

"Yes, we were. He was a good man, Francine." I don't remember if we hugged. If we did, the gulf between us was still there.

Downstairs, people were helping themselves to the roast beef and turkey and salads laid out on the dining room table. I knew it was thanks to Katherine, who had gone grocery shopping yesterday, that the funeral spread was as generous as it was. Otto Simplensky, a friend of Dad's who went back many years, was among the hungry guests. Since Otto was his friend, he could do no wrong in my father's eyes— my father, for whom, like Claire, the world was divided into black and white, loyal and disloyal. From what *I* remember, Otto was a colorful character but a bit of a bigot—and cheap. He never bought his own copy of the *Chicago Sunday Tribune*. Instead, he waited for Dad to bring over *our* paper to his house every Sunday afternoon. I don't think Mom was especially fond of Otto, but she tolerated him for Dad's sake.

Still built like a bull dog but shorter and grayer than I remembered, Otto sought out my mother in the kitchen where she and I were talking. "Well, Helen," he said briskly, "Art's gone. Gone to the bone yard. Looks like you or I will be next. Which one of us do you think will go first?"

Another listener might have missed the wit in my mother's response, but I happened to know she was perfectly capable of a brilliantly timed line. My mother leaned towards him with a beautiful smile. "Otto," she said, looking him straight in the eye, "I think it will be you."

Guests spilled outside. It had rained early that morning. The backyard was green and wet and fresh. *I'm so glad Mom has this*, I thought, breathing the damp, pungent air. I loved this modest plot of land with its shady maple tree and the wobbly statue of St. Francis in the southwest corner, where tiger lilies would soon be blooming. When I visited Joliet on weekends, the backyard was where Mom and I drank our morning coffee when weather permitted.

Perched on the picnic table, I half-listened to fragments of conversations from various groups clustered on the lawn. I could not be sorry my father was dead. Not when he was sick and bedridden and no longer knew Mom. Mom claimed that before he died, he looked at her and smiled. "I *know* my Arthur knew who I was," Mom said. I hoped she was right.

There seemed to be a lot of denial in the family about Dad's mental deterioration. "All Dad needs is a walk around the block once in a while," Lenore declared when it was clear that not only could Dad no longer manage "a walk around the block," but that exercise wasn't going to stop whatever was attacking his mind and memory. I didn't know if it was Alzheimer's. I'd heard of elderly people becoming seriously disoriented due to the slew of pills they took daily—and Dad took a lot of pills: for his blood pressure, his arthritis, his heart. Whatever the case, Katherine and I seemed to be the only ones willing to admit that for the last two years, our father's mental state had grown progressively, gravely, worse.

I thought about my sisters. It was always wonderful to see Katherine, who was as beautiful and stylish as ever. She'd flown in from Connecticut with her husband of four years. Gale, I saw regularly. Through the efforts of an angel-hearted social worker, Gale was now living in a halfway house just north of Chicago and doing better than she had in years. I had no idea what was going through *her* head that day. I knew that in the past, Gale felt hostility towards Dad. I doubted, in truth, that the two of them had ever shared one warm conversation as adults.

There was no love lost between Gale and Claire, either. They were no more compatible now than they'd been as kids. I knew Claire believed Dad's decline was due in large part to the six years that Gale lived with Mom and Dad after she came back from California. *Maybe she's right*, I thought, but what else could Mom have done? I remembered my emaciated sister: the vacant eyes, the drumming fingernails. I wondered if Claire realized how near the brink Gale had been to falling away forever.

I was still on decent terms with Lenore and Myra, although not close with either sister. They were both married and had kids—Lenore, five, Myra, three. They had much more in common with each other than with me. Myra and I had enjoyed a wonderful friendship when I was in college and she was working at an office in Chicago. Our age difference no longer mattered. We played tennis together and shopped for clothes and watched *Charlie's Angels* every week, making catty remarks about Farrah. But after Myra moved to Chicago, I was suddenly the little sister again. If I was with Myra and one or two other sisters, she'd joke about having to censor the conversation because "the little one" was in the room. "Oooh, we mustn't talk about *s-e-x*. The little one's with us!" She was still using that bit when I was in my late twenties.

I never told Myra how much that bothered me; I didn't want to seem like a poor sport. If I *had* said something, she would probably have been exasperated over my sensitivity, although Myra could be plenty sensitive herself, crying readily over hurt feelings. Anyway, it didn't matter now. I rarely saw Lenore or Myra. I wouldn't have been surprised if both sisters regarded my life and the choices I'd made with bemusement: thirty-seven, no marriage, no children. The single sister who never attended their children's birthday parties and rarely said yes to a holiday invite.

It was true that over the years, I'd refused a lot of family invitations. I worked full time; my Saturdays were precious. Spending them at a child's birthday party in a suburb was not my idea of fun. Plus I knew that neither Lenore nor Myra had any idea how long it took to travel from Chicago to Glen Ellyn or Shorewood using public transportation.

Nevertheless, I sometimes suffered guilt attacks for not being a better aunt. Marc only got impatient when I told him this. "Guilty for *what?* Do you seriously think your nephew is going to look back one day and feel traumatized that you weren't at his ninth birthday party? You've got to stop kowtowing to your older sisters, Frannie. They say jump, and you jump."

"I do not! You know perfectly well I have a mind of my own."

"You do, but not around them. I see how you act, and I see how they act. I saw it the first time I went down to Joliet with you. When we were through with dinner, you were the only one to help your mother clear the table. *I* took my plate to the kitchen. Lenore sat there like a queen. And it wasn't because she was busy with her children. Margie waited on those kids hand and foot the whole night."

Claire had said similar things when we were still best friends. I used to talk with her on the phone every day at work. We loved discussing our family. *Gossiping* about our family, really. Claire's observations were opinionated and trenchant and funny. Then they began to strike me as uncomfortably caustic. She had three small children and a husband who worked at least sixty hours a week at one of the largest and busiest law firms in Chicago. Being an extremely intelligent, musically gifted woman, Claire must have felt terribly isolated—and insulated—sometimes, no matter how much she adored her husband and children. If only I had thought about her situation with a little more compassion, I would never have lectured her the way that I did.

I called Claire one Friday morning from work and announced that I was tired of the way she talked about other family members. It was unnecessary and sometimes mean-spirited, I said, zealous in the manner of people who know they're right. I didn't consider how much those words would hurt my sister.

A week after righteously chiding her, I called. I was more nervous than I thought I would be when she answered. "Hi, Claire! It's

Frannie. Listen, it feels like forever since we talked. I know we had a bad conversation last time. I wanted to know how you're doing." I tried to sound casual and breezy, as if nothing *that* bad had taken place between us. Claire let me know immediately this was not going to work.

"I don't think this is the time to discuss what happened, Francine" she informed me coolly. "In fact, I'm no longer comfortable talking to you when you're at work. Essentially, you're stealing money from your employer when you spend time on personal calls. You may call me this weekend, on your own time, if you care to talk."

When Claire called me *Francine* instead of *Frannie*, I felt an unpleasant jolt. I did call her the following Saturday. I should simply have apologized. Instead, I tried to save face. Feeling defensive and even more nervous than I had earlier that week, I explained my point of view and tried to listen to hers. But before long words heavy with hurt and anger were being exchanged between us. Claire demanded to know what she had said that I considered "mean-spirited."

"I don't think it would do any good to bring up stuff from the past—"

"No! You called me that, and I want to know. It's not fair to put something like that out there and then not back it up."

"Well—" I knew I should probably shut up; instead, I plunged in. "Like when you talk about Gale's hair, how she ought to wash it more. How you criticize her teeth. When you talk about Lenore's and Myra's kids. I know Lenore thinks it's cute to make her little girls take those awful photographs where they pose sexy, but they're only five and eight, it's not *their* fault. I'm just not comfortable being that critical about *kids*."

"If it bothered you that much, why didn't you say something at the time?"

"I should have! I should have."

"You've said things *I've* found pretty cold-hearted, Francine. Cruel, actually. Like saying Dad was a man who was not meant to have children. I don't understand how you can say that about your own father."

"You're taking it out of context—"

"Well, you're doing the same!"

Our rift only widened. From that day on, any conversation I had with Claire was absurdly bland. That awful word that I had used—"mean-spirited"—seemed to have burned into her memory. She was not going to risk my calling her that ever again. She was excruciatingly careful to exclude from our conversation anything that was not utterly lacking in interest or controversy. Not surprisingly, we had fewer and fewer conversations. And she never called me *Frannie* again.

Thank God I have Marc, I thought, feeling suddenly heartsick in that backyard on the day of my father's funeral. I'd talked with Katherine about my estrangement from Claire, but there was nothing she could do. It was up to me to mend the damage. But as time passed—it had been seven months since our quarrel—I let Claire's chilly demeanor, her meticulously neutral conversations, convince me I *had* been right, that the Claire I had loved so dearly was gone. I did not even want to be friends with the purposefully bland, self-possessed woman who had replaced her. I certainly did not want to apologize to her.

Guests lingered throughout the afternoon, drinking bottles of imported beer, sipping cups of coffee poured from the big silver urn we used on holidays when I was growing up. It was almost evening when the last of them drove away. Katherine's husband was among them; he was flying home that night. Katherine was staying in Joliet for another two days. I, too, was spending the night; I wanted to be with my mother.

Katherine and I collected dishes and napkins and silverware from the backyard and the living and dining rooms. We cleared the table, took out the three leaves, and put away leftovers. Then, reminiscing with Mom, we washed and dried the dishes. It was not as sad a night as I had expected. Mom had done her grieving months before this day. "I've already cried my tears, honey," she told me not long before Dad passed away. "I want Arthur to be at peace."

I wanted my father to be at peace, too. But I couldn't grieve for him as Claire did. As Katherine and Mom talked in the clean, candle-lit kitchen that night, something my father said to me when I was thirty-four or thirty-five surfaced without warning. "Do you know who's going to keep the family together once your mother and I are gone? Your sister Claire, that's who."

He'd said that on one of my weekend visits home. We had been sitting quietly in the living room, my father and I. I wouldn't have guessed, until he spoke, how those words stung. He had said them as if he were daring me to disagree, as if *my* place in the scheme of the family were completely irrelevant.

I pushed the memory away. I did not want to indulge in petty grievances towards my father on the night of his funeral. I knew down to my bones, as Claire said earlier, that he was a good man. But a nasty star of bitterness exploded inside. *Okay, maybe I won't keep the family together. Maybe I don't attend children's birthday parties and I'm living with a man, Dad. Yeah, I'm shacking up, as you would say. But I'm here now, and the house is in order, and the dishes are done. I'm here now, Dad.*

Margie's Will

've read that much of our character, even our destiny, depends on
where we fit in the family dynamic. The oldest child is most likely
to exhibit leadership qualities, the middle child often gets lost in
the shuffle, the youngest child is spoiled. These are the stereotypes. My
sisters may disagree, but I do not think I was indulged because I was
the youngest. If anything, having grown up in a house where his
brother, Elmer, *was* "the baby," Dad was harder on me.

Still, patterns that might be familiar to psychologists emerge when
I compare myself with my oldest sister, Lenore. I did my best, for example,
to avoid attention from adults. Good or bad, Lenore craved such attention. Holidays centered on huge fights between Mom and Dad and her—
dramas resolved in the nick of time, just before we left for Mass or the
relatives came over. I never had stormy scenes with my parents. Part of
this was because Lenore battled for freedoms that came easily to me. But
another reason was my fear of confrontation. I should have confronted
more. Maybe then, I wouldn't still have dreams of trying to talk to my
father, but not being able to because my lips are shaking so badly. I should
have learned how to stand up for myself when I felt put upon by my sisters
instead of letting hurts fester. I rarely did this.

I was rarely the center of attention, either. My senior year of
college, at the urging of several professors, I applied to graduate school.
I wasn't sure what graduate school enabled you to do, but I applied.

The only university I knew of that was close by was the University of Chicago, so that's where I sent my application and my ten poems (I was applying for English with an emphasis in creative writing). When I was accepted, no one except my mother recognized this was a real accomplishment. Later that spring, I graduated from Joliet's College of Saint Francis. At the restaurant dinner afterwards, Bill and Lenore announced that they were going to have a baby. This sparked a lot more enthusiasm around the table—especially from Margie and Ginny—than my graduating.

I wasn't mad at Lenore for stealing the spotlight. I was used to Margie and Ginny taking more interest in my older sisters than they did in me. If I dropped by for a visit with Katherine or Claire, my aunts talked almost exclusively to the older sister. It had always been that way. Katherine and Gale were both very close to Margie, but I think out of us six girls, my aunt's deepest bond was with Lenore.

Lenore was no shy observer. Although a bespectacled daydreamer in grammar school, by the time she was attending Joliet Junior College, she had blossomed. She was extremely pretty and fun loving, with a keen, practical mind like Margie's, a cheerful nature, and sometimes not a clue as to what was appropriate. When she was nineteen, she invited not one but *two* guys she was currently dating to a family cookout. Each came assuming he was the only one asked. Sitting between the two of them in paisley hip huggers, Lenore was as relaxed as a Southern Belle lounging among her suitors.

Lenore actively sought Margie's advice in matters ranging from student teaching to child rearing. This had to be deeply gratifying to Margie, who loved to offer hands-on help, who needed to be needed. I understand why she couldn't possibly feel the same bond with me. Not only was I quiet and reserved, I prided myself on being self-sufficient. And I was fiercely protective about my writing; I shared it only with my mother. When a number of my poems appeared in the College of Saint Francis's literary journal, I didn't even think of giving Margie a copy of the magazine. It did not occur to me that she might value it. Lenore never questioned that her successes were important to Margie.

As we grew older, Lenore remained part of our aunts' daily lives, grocery shopping for Margie when she was feeling under the weather, stopping by for a quick visit with the kids before supper. She was the Tolf daughter who hadn't moved away, the living link between our family's older and younger generations. And Marjorie adored Lenore's children. She was as involved with their lives as she had been with ours, driving the boys to school when they were young, accompanying the family on summer vacations which she paid for. She was extremely generous to Lenore. I never resented the fact that, over the years, my aunt gave me a fraction of what she gave my oldest sister. I was single, after all, and earned a decent living as a secretary at a small law office. The way I figured it, Margie didn't have to give me anything. I was glad for the Christmas checks, the birthday envelopes.

But the discrepancy was considerable. When I was in my mid thirties, Margie either called or wrote me—I can't remember—saying how much she regretted this, especially since I was her godchild. I responded with a letter telling her how foolish her guilt was. I reminded her about the trips she took Claire and me on when we were in grade school, the many gifts she'd given me. It felt good to write that letter. I knew my Aunt Marjorie was a deeply good, deeply honorable woman with a soul scrubbed as clean as her kitchen floor.

After Margie was diagnosed with borderline diabetes, her one fear was going blind. This never happened. My aunt was active and busy until two weeks before her death. She died peacefully in her sleep at St. Joseph's Hospital. She was eighty-six. I believe her only other hospital admission due to diabetes was about six months earlier. I remember that hospital stay because after taking the train to Joliet the night before, I visited Margie on a Saturday afternoon with Mom.

When we walked into the room, Lenore was telling Margie about her oldest son, who everyone knew was Margie's favorite. "Mikey made the high school golf team, Margie! We're so proud of him. Only thing is, he's gonna be really busy practicing and he's the only boy on the team who doesn't have his own car. It'll be hard drivin' back and forth to Inwood, but we'll have to manage."

Nice, I thought drily. Our aunt is literally lying in a hospital bed and my sister's still working her. I knew this was cynical. I couldn't help it. Lenore's two youngest girls were running up and down the hall outside. A nurse stuck her head in the door. "Someone had better do something with those kids! They're creating havoc."

"Come on in here, girls," Lenore called cheerfully, remaining in her chair next to Margie's bed. "I'm thinkin' if Bill and I could only get our hands on a nice little used car, Margie, that would be perfect."

Margie died that fall. Her funeral mass was extremely well attended—testament to a generous, fully lived life. I did not think I was going to cry, but when Father Flannigan spoke of the many children whose lives were the better for having had Margie as a teacher, tears rolled down my face. How would Ginny manage without Margie? How would Mom?

Margie had asked my mother to be executor of her will. I don't remember what the exact terms of the will were. My aunt left some money to Mom and the bulk of her estate to Ginny. All six of us girls received money as well, a sum divided evenly between us. When Lenore learned there was nothing in Margie's will specifying a larger amount for her alone, she went—in a word—berserk. She accused Mom of destroying a codicil she claimed Margie had added to the original will. *You senile old bitch,* Lenore shouted at our mother in a fit of blind anger. Mom told me this during a telephone conversation. She wasn't crying, but I knew that she had been.

"Jesus *Christ,*" I fumed to Marc afterward, "Lenore got a down payment for a house, probably *two* houses. She got vacations, tuition for her kids, a brand new deck. Margie gave and gave and gave to her. And now she *still* wants more? Unbelievable!"

I did not want anything to do with my oldest sister, and for months, that's how it was. Then, I got a call from Mom. She told me she was finally finishing up with Margie's estate and that she was now free to dispose of her sister's Dodge. It was almost ten years old, but in excellent condition, with very little mileage. "I want you to have it, Frannie," my mother said. "You never asked Margie for anything in your life, and you haven't had a car since you moved to Chicago."

That car couldn't have come at a better time. Marc and I were now living in East Rogers Park. We had moved north because the rent was cheaper, but the nearest grocery store was a mile from our apartment. Marc and I took the train down to Joliet together and drove back in our used Dodge. I hadn't driven for so many years that I was afraid to try, but Marc was happy to be behind a wheel again.

Lenore called me a week later. She couldn't have been sweeter, which immediately set me on guard. After some small talk, she got to the point. "I know Mom gave you Margie's Dodge, Frannie. I just wanted you to know that if you ever were lookin' to get rid of it—"

I cut my sister short. "I'm not looking to get rid of it, Lenore. Marc and I need that car." My voice was shaking. "Before we got it, we were riding the bus eleven blocks to get groceries."

"Okay, Okay! Calm down. I was gonna offer to buy it is all. Take it off your hands in case you didn't want it."

Three days after our phone conversation, I received a letter from Lenore. She wrote that she was very troubled she had upset me; that had never been her intention. She wrote that she was happy I got the car since I obviously needed it. I knew, the way one just knows things sometimes, that her words were sincere.

Lenore was the one sister with whom I had never been particularly close. Eight years made a huge difference when we were growing up, and we still had little in common. I read Tolstoy; Lenore read the *National Enquirer*. I enjoyed spending time by myself; Lenore loved being around people. I shunned conflict, but Lenore thrived on drama, and if conflict was part of the drama, well, it was better than being bored. Yet I sensed in her letter a thread that bound us together: family mattered deeply to Lenore. Even though she had said terrible things to Mom, even though she expected Margie to favor her in her will, good relations with her sisters truly mattered to her.

They mattered to me, too. I hated Claire's and my estrangement. I hated that I no longer knew the woman Myra had become. I put Lenore's letter in a cabinet where I kept other letters I had saved over the years. Inside was the heartbroken note my Aunt Ginny sent me after her cat, Princess, died—three hand-written paragraphs that revealed a sweet, utterly sincere woman very different from the sardonic aunt I knew. There was a letter from John Stobart, a teacher from Joliet Junior College, telling me to believe in my talent as a poet because *he* did. There was correspondence with Claire during the two years she and Rob lived in London. Circumstances had changed so drastically since certain letters were written that I doubted I could ever bring myself to re-read them. But I would never throw them away.

GOLDEN

The summer following Margie's funeral, Gale was struck by a car. Three teenagers in a stolen vehicle attempted to turn from Howard onto Hermitage, where she was walking. They lost control of the car, pinned Gale against a storefront, and fled.

I learned about the hit-and-run accident from Mom, who called me in my apartment in East Rogers Park about 10:00 p.m., eight hours after Gale was taken by ambulance to St. Francis Hospital in Evanston. Hospital staff had just notified my mother, having finally acquired positive identification and a family member's phone number. I was horrified but oddly calm; numbness descends when you get news like that. My mother sounded oddly calm, too. I told her I would be at St. Francis's Intensive Care Unit first thing the next morning.

When I saw Gale, I did not recognize her. The woman lying in the hospital bed was a shattered, bandaged mummy. Machines were hooked up to her body, pumping like great artificial hearts. I learned that her right knee was smashed and bones in her right wrist and left ribs were broken. A lung was punctured. Gale, heavily sedated, lay on the bed with her hospital gown wide open, exposing her breasts.

"I tie it up, but she just undoes it," a nurse told me. "She says she wants the world to know what happened to her." Of course she does, I thought: my sister, who wanted to be a flower when she was four and was now, in her own way, an Amazon warrior—an original even here. I don't remember much about the visit. I held Gale's hand, I talked to her. I promised her she was going to be all right.

I told my mother about Gale's injuries, but kept the worst details to myself. I didn't think Lenore, who had since made up with Mom after her fury over Margie's will, had. She was baffled and a little indignant that our seventy-nine-year-old mother never accompanied her on trips to Evanston to visit Gale.

I understood why Mom could not bring herself to visit her own daughter. Gale had already broken once. The first time it happened, Mom had mustered the strength to fight for her recovery. Now Gale was forty-three and broken all over again. My mother didn't have that kind of strength anymore. I think she knew if she saw her daughter at St. Francis Hospital, she would not be able to survive it.

The truth is, I planned my visits so I would not run into Lenore and Myra, who usually came together. After a day we had spent together three years ago, I vowed to myself I would never be with just the two of them again if I could help it. We had agreed, that day, to visit Gale, who then had a small apartment in Hyde Park. Mom suspected she had started drinking and was not taking her medication. Her fears proved true. Gale's apartment was a pathetic hovel. She hadn't showered or combed her hair in days, and it was clear from the way she spoke that she was slipping away from the real, the present. The day ended with me accompanying Gale in an ambulance to the mental ward of a South Side hospital, then taking an hour and a half worth of trains and buses back to the North Side of Chicago.

That long Saturday was hard enough, but what rankled was the family dynamic that immediately took over once I slipped into the back seat of Lenore's car that morning and the three of us headed to Hyde Park. (Myra had thought my request to be picked up extravagant, but Lenore was willing.) They were the older, wiser sisters; I was the little one. And although she had no way of knowing it, Myra's voice was nearly unbearable to me. She sometimes adopted an overly sweet, overly patient way of talking that she would have hooted at when we were growing up. When she spoke to Gale in that voice, I wanted to smash something. Instead, I took her aside and did what I so seldom had the wisdom or courage to do in a mature way as far as family was concerned: I dealt with it.

"Myra," I said, "this is going to be a difficult day for all of us. We're going to get through it, but not if you keep using that voice. I'm sorry, I know you think it's the right way to talk to Gale, but I cannot stand it." For the rest of the day, Myra spoke normally.

But the dynamic remained, and so—instigated, it seemed to me by Myra—did that subtle "two against one" that can happen in a group of three. Myra had always teased me when I was a kid, but she was also the sister I could talk to about sensitive issues—embarrassments, fears. She knew when *not* to tease. She didn't seem to know anymore; getting the laugh was the important thing. I fumed about that Saturday for days and finally wrote Myra an angry letter. She did not respond. The fierce jolt of pleasure I felt upon dropping my letter in the mailbox eventually thickened into guilt. Why hadn't I simply called my sister? Why was it so hard to talk to her, to tell her when her behavior bothered me? We had been so close when I was in college. Couldn't she understand it hurt to be demoted from a trusted friend to the little sister who was the butt of jokes at family gatherings?

Finally, I called Myra and apologized. She was lovely about it. But she never acknowledged I'd had anything to be upset about. I knew if I found myself in Gale's hospital room with Lenore and Myra, the tired dynamic of older sisters versus youngest sister would take over. I couldn't deal with that *and* Gale. Besides, I wanted Gale to myself. I liked talking to her without worrying about being self-conscious.

Lenore told Mom that doctors said it was doubtful that Gale would walk again. I imagined my sister relating the news, almost relishing the drama of it. I didn't believe Gale would never walk again. I don't know *why*, when I think of the abysmal shape she was in both physically and mentally. But I simply did not believe it. "The hell with what Lenore told you, Mom," I said one night when we were talking on the phone. "I know she's going to walk again. She looks better every time I visit."

Eventually, Gale recognized me when I visited her. I doubt she remembered anything I said an hour after I left, but when I sat beside her bed, she knew me. One evening, she wanted to write a letter to Mom. I took out a pen, found some scratch paper, and wrote down the words my forty-three-year-old bi-polar/schizophrenic/cast- and bandage-encased sister dictated:

Dear Mom,
      I am doing better. Margie is an angel and watches over me. She is above the TV. There is a puppy at the foot of my bed. (For weeks, Gale mistook the pumping of the machines for a puppy.) *Francine has been—* she paused for a long time, as if she'd forgotten how to say what she wanted. Finally she decided on . . . *a Good Egg.* (She asked me to capitalize this.) *I love you.*
      Gale

I sent the letter to Mom along with a note of my own. I told her that I, too, felt Margie's presence in the room. This wasn't true, but I knew it would comfort my mother. And I did feel something during my visits with Gale at St. Francis Hospital. Not my aunt's presence, but sometimes a warmth, a feeling of being embraced. If I had to assign that feeling a color—the way I assigned certain words colors when I was a kid—I would say it was golden.

EAST ROGERS PARK

One evening after I visited Gale and came home, Marc walked into the dining room and found me sitting with my head in my hands.

"Frannie, you don't have to visit Gale every night. You work full time. It's too much."

"I don't visit her every night. It's not that. I'm just tired."

"You want some scrambled eggs? Or I could make you a grilled cheese. You need to eat something." Marc loved to cook. He would rather have offered angel hair pasta with fresh pesto than grilled cheese, but he knew my favorites. *You can take the girl out of Joliet, but you can't take Joliet out of the girl,* he'd tell me with affection. Marc and I fought plenty, but I never doubted he loved me. That love was the cornerstone of my adult life. From the very start, when I'd met him at twenty-seven, I knew I could be myself with Marc. I didn't need to pretend I was less intelligent or less passionate about books and animals and nature than I was. Marc didn't think it was selfish or strange that I didn't want children. He accepted me for the way I was—and he *listened.* He listened as only my mother did. And Claire, before our friendship fell apart.

"Thank you, Marco. Maybe later. I just feel like sitting here right now."

I *was* tired, but it wasn't that, either. I could hear the *pop pop pop* of teenagers setting off cherry bombs at the beach less than a quarter of a mile away. Our apartment building bordered a park at the edge of Lake Michigan. The park must have been beautiful once. Now it was strewn with trash. Even the trees had gang graffiti.

We were living in this neighborhood because of me. Our apartment on Cornelia Street in Chicago's Belmont Harbor neighborhood was lovely, with brand new hardwood floors, shining kitchen appliances, and a screened-in sun deck. I fell in love with it the minute I stepped inside. Unfortunately, neighbors ruined the little paradise it could have been. The guy above us loved disco. The pounding began at 7:00 a.m. and sometimes went on for hours. Across the courtyard, a kid who looked like he was just out of college blasted heavy metal. One night when they were both at it, I felt as desperate as I ever had in my life. "We have to move," I said to Marc. "I don't care how expensive it's going to be. I have to get the fuck out of this apartment!"

It *was* expensive to break that lease—and once we began apartment hunting, we soon learned we could no longer afford to live in Belmont Harbor. Marc worked temporary jobs; my secretary's salary was the only one we could count on. We looked farther north, finally settling on a place in East Rogers Park. It was large, at least, and seemed quiet enough. East Rogers Park had once been a spacious, affluent neighborhood. There were some elegant pockets left in it, but the majority of the area had declined—radically.

I tried hard to love my new neighborhood. In the end, I couldn't. I hated the litter, the boarded-up storefronts, the grimy windows of the liquor store on Morse Avenue, just under the El platform. I hated the half-eaten fast food and empty liquor bottles left by homeless people who slept in the park. Sometimes they slept right outside our living room window. And they left more than food and bottles: used tampons, urine-soaked clothing. I'd go out on Saturday with gloves and a plastic garbage bag and handle things I never thought I would be able to touch. Once Marc and I had to haul a soiled, rain-soaked mattress to the dumpster.

And I hadn't escaped noise after all. Our bedroom looked out on a narrow walkway between apartment buildings. Directly across from us lived an old man who watched TV—loudly—every night until the small hours. We might as well have had the television in our own room. The only way to not hear it was to shut the window and turn our ancient air conditioner to blast.

I learned during the eighteen months we spent in East Rogers Park how living in an economically depressed neighborhood frays your nerves; how seeing trash piled against curbs and scattered across yards morning after morning after morning diminishes your spirit. I was scared we would never get out, but part of me thought, why should we be the lucky ones? I could imagine my sister Katherine's impatience with this kind of thinking. "For God sake, Frannie, wanting to get out of a bad neighborhood is hardly being selfish. Where do you *get* these ideas? Tell Marc he better find a job fast. I don't want my beautiful, brilliant sister living in a ghetto. You deserve to be happy. When are you going to understand that?"

Did I really think I didn't deserve to be happy? How could that be when I had always felt lucky for how *little* it took? I didn't need a house and a yard, or jewelry, or vacations. I had Marc, my health, my two cats. I had Lake Michigan, the seals at Lincoln Park Zoo, a used book store on Clark Street where four tabbies lounged among the stacks. If only I could be assured of quiet in my own home, I wouldn't ask for anything more. "You're the one daughter I never worry about," my mother had said to me a few months ago. "You know what to treasure, Frannie. I know you'll always be all right."

I sat at the dining room table listening to the cherry bombs' ugly staccato. It sounded like gunfire. *My very own Sarejevo sound track,* I thought drily. I rarely walked through the park that was right outside my window; it depressed me too much. But last weekend, I had. I'd seen a woman sitting on a bench drinking a bottle of Wild Irish Rose at two in the afternoon. In the heat of summer, she wore a winter coat and laceless tennis shoes, avoiding my gaze when I passed her. That poor soul was once a little girl, I'd thought. She'd had the silky skin all little girls have, and big, grave eyes that weren't ashamed to gaze up at anyone. I imagined her noticing clouds in puddles and the way gravel sparkled like diamonds. She wanted to be a ballerina and a zookeeper and a scientist when she grew up.

I had not written a line of poetry in years, but the contrast between the child I imagined and the ravaged woman on the park bench made me ache to capture it in a poem. Instead, I tucked the image away as I had others since moving: a riot of sunflowers climbing skyward from the cracks of asphalt; a Latina girl who might have been seventeen kissing her baby's nose again and again as she waited on the Morse Avenue platform for the El.

One cool, windy morning, I woke to the sound of waves pounding the beach and the sweet jangle of wind chimes. The elderly lady who lived above us hung a set of them from the roof of her back porch. She also had window boxes filled with ruffly pink flowers.

"They're so pretty," I told her when we met in the lobby. "What are they?"

"Begonias, dear. They don't need much tending. A little water and a little light and they bloom all summer."

SEPTEMBER

That August, my mother called Lenore one evening and asked if she would drive her to St. Joseph's Hospital. She felt very tired and weak, she said. When Lenore told me about this, I was not overly worried. I figured Mom needed rest and would be released in a few days.

But when Marc and I visited her at the hospital the next day, I knew she was sicker than I had thought. Mom's voice and manner lacked all vitality. Standing by her bed with Marc, I was at a loss of what to say to my own mother.

"We brought you a *Sunday Tribune*," Marc said, putting the thick newspaper on her tray.

Mom talked listlessly of finding a condo; the house was too big and a burden to keep up. "You could move in with Ginny," I said, and immediately regretted it. I *knew* my mother did not want to live with her sister, whose bungalow was filling with clutter that Ginny refused to throw away. Why had I suggested this? Mom was never going to move. 206 South Raynor Avenue had been her home for more than forty years.

When I think of that time now—the end of the summer of 1997—it is a blur of hospital visits. Visits to Gale, visits to Earl, my boss of eleven years who was dying of melanoma, visits to Mom. I did not feel confident driving, so Marc had to take me to Joliet and, later, to

Glen Ellyn to see her. He wasn't happy with his role as chauffeur. "I don't understand how you can be scared of driving, Frannie! It's like riding a bike. It comes right back."

But I *was* scared. I hadn't driven in over fifteen years. I could not imagine handling that Dodge by myself on the highway. Perhaps some of my fear had to do with the fact that it had been way too long since I'd stepped outside of my comfort zone in *any* way. I had worked at the same small law firm for eleven years. I had my weekly routine, my quiet weekends. If my life was unexciting, it was also safe and familiar. The one risk I had taken—moving—landed me in a neighborhood I longed to get out of.

Doctors told my mother that going back home was out of the question; she needed help. Both Lenore and Myra offered to take care of Mom. Claire probably did, too. Our mother ended up staying with Myra. Her household was much less chaotic than Lenore's, and Glen Ellyn was considerably closer to Joliet than Glencoe, where Claire lived. Myra's oldest son gave up his bedroom so Mom could have a room to herself. When Myra and her husband, Paul, brought Mom home from the hospital, they and their kids welcomed her with a hand-made sign hung above the door of her room. Myra had brought personal items from Mom's house and scattered them throughout so Mom would feel more at home.

After learning about this from Katherine, I called Myra to tell her what a wonderful thing she was doing for Mom. It was not a comfortable conversation. A coolness in my sister's voice told me she felt I had somehow failed to do my part.

Mom stayed at Myra's house for less than two weeks before Myra had to call an ambulance to take her back to the hospital. I don't know how often Myra and Lenore visited Mom during her second hospital stay, but I know it was considerably more than I did. I was sure they believed this was due to selfishness on my part. *I work full time, I live in Chicago, I have to depend on Marc for rides and he thinks I visit TOO much*, I'd tell myself, angry for being manipulated into guilt—but guilty nonetheless.

My mixed emotions only frustrated Marc. "What have you done to feel guilty? You love your mother. Why do you do this to yourself?" I knew why. Because I was the youngest, and when an older sister disapproved of my actions, I still felt I was the one who had to be wrong. Metal in Myra or Lenore's voice could turn me into an insecure, contrite eight-year-old. It was ridiculous. It was *shameful*. I did not share this insight with Marc.

August turned into September, the month Mom used to sing about. She loved the deep blue skies and golden air, the heavy foliage just beginning to ripen to yellow. On the second day of my mother's favorite month, Marc picked me up after work and we drove down to Joliet. Lenore knew I was planning to visit Mom. She wanted me to call her once I was at St. Joseph's so we could see her together. I didn't call Lenore. I wanted to be alone with my mother. As I sat by her bed in the IC unit, I knew she did not know me, but I hoped she somehow realized that someone who loved her was near. Her breathing was shallow; it sounded as if it hurt her. Numerous tubes were hooked up to her body. A doctor had said all of Mom's organs were closing down.

I helped my mother drink some water. It was difficult for her. Some of the water from the paper cup dribbled down her hospital gown, which opened in front. Adjusting it, I saw my mother's naked body for the first time: the bloated belly and thin pubic hair, the purple bruises on her thighs. Something inside of me opened and deepened then. I did not cry as I covered my mother as gently as possible. I asked God to let her die in peace and without pain.

The next morning, I walked into Schneider and Schneider and was told by Maribel, a secretary I'd worked with for ten years, that our boss, Earl, had passed away. Maribel and Dez were trying not to cry as phones rang and Earl's son attempted to dictate his father's obituary. In the midst of this havoc, Lenore called. She said I had better come to the hospital right away.

"*Now?* I was there last night, and my boss just died—"

"All I can tell you is that Mom is not doing at all well. But you do what you think is best."

After I hung up the phone, I wasn't as alarmed as someone else might have been upon hearing those words. I knew Lenore exaggerated. *Constantly.* Still, despite what a terrible time it was to desert the office, I decided I had better find a way to get to Joliet. Marc was working. I could not ask him once again to make the double trip. The easiest way for me to get there was to take the train, but once I was at the station, how was I going to get to the hospital? I called Claire and told her of Lenore's call. Lenore had called her as well. I asked her if there was any way she could pick me up.

"No," Claire said thoughtfully. "It really is out of the way, Francine. Picking you up would add forty-five minutes to the trip, probably more. You can take the train to Wilmette. I'll meet you at the station."

It took almost an hour to get to Wilmette—the last stop, going north, of the Evanston Express, and the opposite direction of Joliet. But once I was there, Claire's minivan was waiting. What I remember about our drive to the hospital was how self-possessed Claire seemed. She had the classical station playing loudly. At one point, while listening to a piece, Claire murmured to herself, "That sounds like Mendelssohn." When the announcer named the composer—who was, indeed, Mendelssohn—Claire smiled. "There. I knew I was right."

But being on the brink of a loved one's death can make for strange behavior. For all I know, Claire thought *I* was the inexplicably self-possessed sister. When we got to the hospital, I took the time to go the bathroom, comb my hair, and slip in a pair of earrings. *Why*, I ask myself now. How could it possibly have mattered to me how I looked?

When I saw my mother lying in the hospital bed, I knew she had died. I thought Claire understood this, too. She took Mom's hand and began, in a tearful voice, to talk to her. A nurse slid open the curtain separating Mom's bed from others in the IC unit. "Oh, I apologize, ladies! I'm so sorry for your loss. I'll give you back your privacy so you can say good-bye to your mother."

Claire turned to the nurse with a sound that was half sob and half a hysterical laugh. "You—you mean she's dead?"

"Yes, dear. She died this morning. Two daughters were with her the whole time. She died peaceful, honey."

We spent our last moments with our mother. Claire asked me if I would call Lenore to tell her we were coming over to her house, which was only about ten minutes away. I found a pay phone and dialed Lenore's number. When I heard her voice at the other end, I could hardly speak. "We're at the hospital, Lenore," I whispered. "Mom's dead."

"I know she's dead, Francine," my sister replied. "I was there. What do *you* care? The office is more important to you than your own mother."

When I picture that moment in my mind, I see myself sinking to the floor and hugging my knees tight. I don't know if I did this. On the way over to Lenore's, Claire reminded me in a cool voice that it was *Lenore* we had to think about; she and Myra had been through a heartbreaking morning. I knew this. It only made my sense of isolation worse. I remember the tall stacks of *Cosmopolitans* in Lenore's living room, how Claire and I had to navigate our way around them. I remember Claire hugging Lenore warmly, Lenore's hasty apology to me. "It's all right," I said numbly, "I'm glad you were there."

A death in the family makes for work you don't realize needs to be done until it happens. The rest of the afternoon was filled with telephone calls and planning and errands. Claire drove home shortly before five o' clock. I stayed with Lenore to go through Mom's closet and choose what clothes she would be buried in. Then Lenore drove me to the train station for the milk run back to Chicago.

I was still numb when I called home from a pay phone outside LaSalle Street Station. I got the answering machine instead of Marc. "Mom's dead. I'm at the train station. I'll be home as soon as I can," I said, sounding harsher than I wanted to. I was angry he had not answered; I had so needed his voice. I took Ravenswood El, transferred at Belmont, waited for the Howard, rode past ten stops to Morse Avenue, then walked three and a half blocks through East Rogers Park to our apartment on Farwell Avenue. I had been calm and helpful and exquisitely polite the entire day. When I opened the door and saw Marc, I started to cry.

The next day, we met at Fred Dames Funeral Home to discuss our mother's funeral arrangements. It seems likely *now* that when I said hello to Myra in the parking lot and she turned her back to me, she simply did not hear me. It seems likely *now* that when the four of us— myself, Claire, Myra and Lenore—sat down in the funeral director's office and Myra pulled her chair away from me and towards Lenore, she was not doing it to hurt me. But grief and guilt are a horrific combination. They make you more than a little paranoid. They also make you anxious to assign blame to someone else. In the days after Mom's death, I felt wounded by such slights without ever considering how difficult the morning of our mother's death must have been for Myra and Lenore. That would have forced me to see them at their best, and I didn't want to do that.

Yet it did not occur to me until years after Mom's death that Lenore and Myra were in fact the fortunate sisters. They got to be there when our mother passed away. This was a gift, not a burden. I don't know how the chemistry might have changed during their vigil if I had been sitting alongside them at Mom's bed. I know that Myra kept assuring our mother over and over that all of us loved her.

"Lenore loves you. Katherine loves you. I love you. Gale loves you. Claire loves you. Frannie loves you. Laffie loves you." (Laffie was Mom's little poodle.)

"I know, I know," Mom half-whispered, half-groaned at one point. Lenore could not hold back an eruption of gallows laughter when she related this some days after the funeral. All I could think was, *Jesus, I hope Myra did not use that sweet, syrupy voice. Don't let that be the last thing my mother heard.*

Katherine was in Milan the day Mom died. As the buyer of women's clothing for an exclusive store in Greenwich, she was viewing couture lines. Katherine flew back to New York. Then she and her husband flew to Chicago. She had assumed that she and David could stay at Mom's house, but Lenore refused to give her the key. I had no idea why. Surely Lenore did not think Katherine was going to steal something—the idea was laughable. I suspected Katherine and Lenore had had words after Lenore's fury over Margie's will. Katherine adored Mom and was fiercely protective of her. She told me more than once that the only time she had ever heard Mom cry was when she repeated what Lenore had called her.

We got through the wake and the funeral mass at St. Patrick's, my four sisters and I. Gale was still hospitalized from her hit-and-run accident. I had assumed, when discussing the matter with Myra and Lenore days before, that the funeral dinner would be held at our mother's house. But the idea shocked them; they said it was ghoulish. Instead, Claire hosted the dinner. Since she and her husband lived in Glencoe—fifty miles from Joliet—it turned out to be a strictly family affair.

Katherine, who was jetlagged and probably hadn't slept in two days, drank too much wine and ended up sobbing on her husband's shoulder, then mine. She was mortified about it afterwards. "Don't be," I said during a telephone conversation a few days later. "So you had a little too much to drink. What matters is that you loved Mom, and you are in her heart. Always."

"Darling Frannie. Mom loved you best, you know."

"No, no! Mom didn't have favorites."

"Maybe not. But she had a special bond with you. Francine, listen to me. Don't burden yourself with guilt that is needless and stupid. Who *cares* if you weren't there when Mother died? You were there for her every day of your life. Don't you think that's more important?"

No, I didn't give a damn if Katherine drank too much wine at the funeral dinner. Even with Marc, even knowing how much I did love Mom, I couldn't have gotten through that day without her.

FALLOUT

I knew it would not be long before we were back at St. Patrick's for the last funeral. By the time of Mom's death, Ginny was a resident of Rosedale Nursing Home. At first, she spoke of eventually returning to her bungalow on Hunter Avenue. But she was never going back there. Each time I visited, my aunt was weaker and more forgetful. She barely showed any emotion when my sisters and I visited after Mom's funeral.

My aunt worried about her two cats, however, and in deference to this—and also because of pressure from Lenore, who was taking care of them at Ginny's house—I decided on a trial adoption. Part of my decision was guilt—naturally, guilt!—over not taking Laffie, Mom's poodle. Years ago, I had promised my mother I'd take care of him after she died. It seemed an easy promise at the time, and I meant it. But Marc and I now lived in a building where dogs were not allowed. Even if I got around that rule, we already had two cats and both of us worked. I was relieved and thankful when Myra and Paul—who had their own small dog and a large backyard—offered to take our mother's gentle little dog.

Marc was not happy over my decision to take in two more cats. "Why did you let your sister pressure you into this? I'm not living in an apartment with four cats! That's crazy." It took a lot of persuasion before Marc finally gave in—as I knew he would—and we drove down to Joliet to pick up Smokey and Queen.

I tried my best to make it work. For two weeks, Marc and I dealt with four felines circling one another warily. We dealt with hisses and earsplitting screams and our cats—*our* cats—being chased under the bed by Smokey, who was affectionate with humans but terrorized his own kind. But when I came home one evening to find my little black cat, Sheeba, cowering in a cabinet above the refrigerator as Queen, Ginny's Siamese, watched her from below with two malevolent slits of turquoise, I knew Marc was right—this could not go on. Marc and I returned Ginny's cats to Joliet.

Ginny passed away the following January of 1998, four months after Mom's death. A fourth wake was held at Fred Dames Funeral Home; a fourth funeral mass was led by Father Flannigan at St. Patrick's Church. "Let's just try to get through this day," I heard Myra murmur to Lenore at the wake.

It turned out to be quite a day to get through. We had agreed, my sisters and I, to meet at Margie's and Ginny's bungalow after the burial. Ginny had not made out a will; we needed to discuss how to handle this. Claire was originally executor of my aunt's estate. She had a law degree, after all, and was meticulously honest. She had executed Mom's will without a hitch. I figured she would navigate her way around probate just as smoothly.

Lenore, however, had insisted that this time, *she* be named executor. Perhaps she had even gone to court—I don't remember. All I know is that Lenore was running the show when we gathered in Margie's and Ginny's living room at 6 South Hunter. Marc and the brothers-in-law, having gone to buy coffee and donuts and deposited them in the dining room, got the hell out of there. I didn't blame them. The air held so much tension it crackled.

Lenore began by asking each of us if there was anything special we wanted to take from our aunt's house. I chose the oil painting of Pilcher Park that hung above the mantle. Someone else wanted the hurricane lamp, someone else the fish platter. Voices were clipped but polite. Then—I don't remember how it happened—all hell broke loose. We all talked at once. Of all things, Lenore was furious with *me* for never having obtained a copy of the police report of Gale's hit-and-run accident. ("Irresponsible!" I remember her shout, pointing an accusing finger at me like someone in a movie. The truth is, I *had* obtained a copy of the report, and had called the police about their chances of catching the three teens who had fled, but I had no intention of handing over ammunition to my trouble-making sister.) Katherine was furious at Lenore for denying her the key to the house she had grown up in. Myra burst into tears because of a note I sent her after Mom's funeral, telling her that I was grateful she had been there for our mother, but she did not have the right to slight me. "It came on my b-birthday," she sobbed. "How can this be happening?"

"There!" Lenore cried. "You see? Myra is the only one in this room who has any *heart*. The only one of my sisters with any compassion. The rest of you should be ashamed of yourselves!"

"Never mind the lecture, Lenore," Claire said calmly. "When can we see Ginny's checking account? I want to know what checks you've written. We all have a right to know."

"You can drop that snotty-ass tone with me, Claire. I may not be a lawyer, but I understand money. And Ginny knew it. Ginny trusted me. That's why she turned over all of her assets to *me*. That's right, girls. The money's in my name!"

Claire held her own with Lenore, looking her levelly in the eye. "And what do you plan to do with it, Lenore?" Looking back, I am amazed Claire reacted as steadily as she did, for she knew the amount of money involved—over three hundred thousand dollars. I had no idea Ginny died with this much in her possession. I should have remembered that she inherited not only the bulk of Margie's estate, but also the bulk of Lucille's, for our Aunt Lucille, who died a wealthy woman, split what she had between Margie and Ginny.

"Oh, you don't have to worry. *I'm* not greedy. I did this to save us the cost of probate. I was going to cut checks for all of you by the end of the week, but I'm not so sure now. It would serve everyone right—except Myra—to make you wait."

Katherine, who was white with anger, did not say a word. Neither did Claire. Instead, she turned her back on Lenore and walked to the kitchen while I apologized to Myra. I was more appalled I'd made her cry than I was over the money situation.

Those few minutes Claire spent by herself in the kitchen were well spent. When she returned to the living room, she was composed and articulate, although her voice trembled slightly. When she was younger, Claire had stuttered. She still did as an adult sometimes if the moment was particularly emotional. But there was no stammering today.

"Lenore," she said, "you and I both know that Virginia was not competent to make the decision about her estate that she did. You still have time to do the right thing while there is some hope of salvaging good will in our family. You can clear up any doubts by dividing the money promptly and sending us all checks for our share. But I promise you on behalf of me and my sisters that if I do not see immediate signs of good faith on your part, Rob and I will take legal action."

"Do whatever the hell you want, Claire. *Legally*, I don't have to give you or anyone else in this room one penny. I inherited it all!"

At first it appeared that Lenore *was* going to act honorably. She hired an attorney—a very decent woman, I remember—who assured Myra and Claire that the money would be divided equally among the six of us. But by July, Lenore had fired her and hired a new attorney. And Claire got wind of the fact that he was transferring Ginny's accounts into Lenore's name.

Claire and Rob took legal action. They hired a Joliet law firm to file suit against Lenore, with the rest of us sisters named as plaintiffs. During the discovery process, we learned that on or near the day our aunt died, Lenore wrote herself a check from Ginny's account for thirty thousand dollars. I don't know if she intended to write any more such checks. I think Lenore was truly convinced that our aunt, who in her last days had sunk into dementia, wanted her—the niece who had never left Joliet, the niece whose kids Margie liked best—to have the lion's share of the estate. Lenore had never stopped believing in a codicil to Margie's will, the codicil she accused our mother of destroying.

In August of 1999, about a year after the lawsuit was filed, the case was heard in court. Claire and Myra testified. I was there for moral support—a little ironic, since my relationship with both Myra and Claire was at best shaky. This time, I drove to Joliet by myself. I had finally mustered the courage to take driving lessons. I was sick of being dependent on others, sick of my own fear. All three of us pulled into the parking lot within a few minutes of one another. I changed from my flats into a pair of modest heels and stepped out of the car, unsure of the reception I would get from my sisters. But on that day, there was solidarity among us.

Claire appeared cool-headed but edgy when she testified. Myra was sincere, earnest, and believable. Lenore, who was still a pretty woman but had put on a bit of weight since her Miss Agriculture days, acted like a middle-aged prom queen, mincing to the stand and tossing her newly blond hair. During a court recess, I ran smack into my oldest sister in the second floor bathroom.

Pure spite I had not felt since the afternoon of Ginny's funeral surfaced without warning. I remembered the terrible name Lenore called Mom and what she said to me at the hospital. I thought about a day that Marc and I drove to Joliet to pick up the oil painting and a few other items from Margie and Ginny's bungalow. When we walked in, it looked as if thieves had ransacked the house. In room after room, I waded through ankle-deep paper work. Contents of cabinets and dresser drawers were dumped on the floor.

"Who could have done this?" I whispered to Marc. "It looks like a rampage."

"Or like somebody told her kids to find a codicil," Marc said drily.

Marc's insights about my sisters were usually correct, but that day I refused to believe him. Lenore couldn't have done this, I told him. She loved Margie. She knew the pride Margie took in her home. When I asked Lenore about the chaos, she agreed it was shocking. Neighborhood kids must have broken in, she said.

Standing a few feet from Lenore in the courthouse's ice cold, air-conditioned bathroom, I wondered about that rather casual explanation.

Had Lenore been so desperate to find some nonexistent codicil that she was willing to trash Margie's house? She didn't appear desperate now. Turning her back to me, she fluffed her hair in the mirror, pursing her lips a little. The way she dismissed my presence infuriated me. *I want to rattle this bitch,* were the exact words that popped into my head.

"May I ask you a question, Lenore?" I said sweetly.

Lenore met my eyes in the mirror. "What is it?"

"How does it feel to have not one but *three* chins?"

"Oh, I can't believe—" Lenore broke off and looked away, surprised and hurt. She hadn't expected such nastiness from me. I didn't care. I laughed, or pretended to laugh, and walked out of the bathroom. Me, the would-be poet. Lover of beauty.

We won the case. The money ended up being distributed evenly among me and my five sisters, although it took another year before Gale got her share. Gale received Social Security Disability, and there were strict rules about how much personal income a resident of Greenwood Care could have. Myra was so worried Gale would be put out on the street that she called Greenwood's director to tell him about Gale's inheritance. She urged Gale to give her share of Ginny's estate to the government. Myra stated this in a brief note to Gale, which the rest of us sisters got copies of. I knew Myra was only looking out for Gale's best interests, but I thought her phone call was rash and her insistence that Gale give up her inheritance premature.

I didn't care for her solution, either. Myra proposed that the rest of us contribute regularly to a pool so that when Gale needed new art supplies or clothes, all she had to do was ask. Again, I knew Myra meant well. But her plan reduced Gale to a charity case, dependent on sisters for small luxuries the rest of us needed no one's permission to buy.

On the other hand, it was absolutely true that Gale had no concept of money and squandered it when she had any. If someone had given Gale a thousand dollars, she would readily have handed it over the following day to a "psychic" so she could meet a handsome poet who would fall in love with her. And Myra was right; Gale could not risk losing her SSI. If she did, Greenwood would cost close to $2,500 a month. But I knew in my gut there had to be a way she could keep money legally.

Claire saw the situation as a family problem to be presided over with her in charge. She began leaving me phone messages informing me that I was to come to her house the following weekend or next Monday evening so she and Myra and I could discuss Gale's future. Those messages, dispensed with a school mistress's authority, made me tighten my hands into fists as I listened to them after I came home from work. I was forty-one years old and a legal secretary at a top-ten law firm in Chicago, a job that was more stressful and demanding than I could ever have imagined when I applied for it—a job, I thought angrily, that Claire couldn't handle for one day—and I was being treated like a wayward child.

I ignored Claire's messages and found an attorney myself for Gale. She set up a Special Needs Trust with me named as guardian. It was perfectly legal and surprisingly uncomplicated: so much for the pro bono lawyer at Rob's firm—perhaps the third largest law firm in the world—telling me in a dismissive voice that there was no way my sister could keep her inheritance.

I also decided, over the course of the next year, to apply for graduate school. I hadn't gone on to the University of Chicago where I'd been accepted twenty years ago. It was too expensive, and at twenty-two I had no idea what I really wanted. Yet I loved my years at Joliet Junior College and the College of St. Francis. I knew classes about Kate Chopin and Emily Dickinson weren't preparing me for the real world. They would never, as my father reminded me, get me a job. But reading and talking about literature made me *happy*.

At forty-two, I still didn't know what I wanted. But I had been working as a secretary for nearly twenty years; it was time for a change. For the past two years, I had been writing poetry seriously, sparked by a class I'd taken at the Newberry Library after Mom died. I think I enrolled in that class because I felt my bearings slipping away. The family closeness I'd known as a child was gone. My friendship with Claire was over, and my mother was dead. I grabbed onto a branch that was still rooted deep enough to support the weight of my loss and my longing—poetry.

Marc and I moved to Manhattan, Kansas, the small, pretty town where Kansas State University is located, in August of 2001. I wanted to forget the fighting and heartache that had occurred between me and my sisters over the past few years. I was tired of analyzing it, sick of being overcome, by turns, with resentment or guilt. *We all made mistakes. We've all moved on. Let it go*, I told myself.

But there were fragments I didn't know what to do with. Just days before Myra contacted Greenwood Care and the question of Gale's inheritance became yet another issue dividing me from Myra and Claire, Claire called me. We'd had a number of telephone conversations since the court ruled in our favor, none of them warm. In fact, several of Claire's notes to me regarding Gale ("Gale Tolf" is how Claire referred to her own sister in these letters) were unapologetically cold. But this day, her voice was different. She was *Claire* again.

"Frannie," she said, "I want to end the ridiculous feud between us. It's gone on too long." I was so astonished, I had to sit down.

"Claire, this is wonderful of you. I know this phone call couldn't have been easy. I want you to know how much it means." We did not talk for long—we were both unpracticed with our new roles as friends. At least I was. I told Claire I would call her soon.

I had every intention of doing so, but I wanted to be ready. I wanted to be sure, when I called, that my own voice was free of bitterness. Claire and I had put each other through a lot of pain. Intellectually, I knew I was at least as much to blame as she was, but my heart still cried, *My god how she hurt me.*

I waited too long. Within a week, I received Myra's note in the mail. The next call I got from Claire was an authoritative message directing me to come to her house to discuss the situation. I think she was angry and hurt that I hadn't called. Her voice was cool steel. And I was Francine, not Frannie.

❧Part Three❧
Halcyon Days

HALCYON DAYS

My sister Gale still regards her twenty-seventh summer as an idyllic season, a golden period when planets were perfectly aligned to assure pleasurable days and passionate nights. Saturn's Return was a mere shadow on the border of her astrological chart—which is another way of saying that the psychotic episodes that were to be diagnosed as schizophrenic came later.

Gale still believes firmly that Saturn's Return caused them. She also believes in tarot cards, astral projection, demons disguised as human beings, and a host of deities ranging from St. Rita to Aphrodite. My sister keeps in touch with all of them; she's a woman who covers her bases. She might lament (proudly) that there's no earth in her chart, but the fact is that in matters she cares about, she's eminently practical. I kid her about that nowadays when we talk on the phone. We're very close, Gale and I. We have the same oddball sense of humor, cackling together like a couple of gleeful crones over some incident no one else would find funny.

We never laughed like that during the summer of 1981 when Gale was twenty-seven and I, a naïve twenty-two-year-old, yanked up my Midwestern roots with trembling fingers and flew to Monterey to spend some time with my bohemian sister. It wasn't that we fought or disliked each other. But I was a stranger in a strange land those five months I lived with Gale, a misfit in a rickety-tickety kingdom where she reigned supreme in a wobbly Victorian house whose kitchen was strung with Christmas lights. Orange nasturtium tangled their way around the back door, which was the entrance everyone used.

Which *sounds* charming. There was a gnarled fig tree in the back-yard, and if I stepped out on the front porch at night, I could hear seals barking on rocks by the pier. But the house my sister rented was falling apart, and Gale was a slob. A stunning slob. The afternoon I arrived, she was not yet home from her part-time job as an art teacher at a senior cit-izen home. I looked around the half-red, half-yellow painted kitchen with its folding table covered with jars of paint brushes, books, a marijuana plant, spilled change, roach clips, and dirty dishes. I looked closer. There was a carrot, no, *two* carrots rotting on the floor under the table, stuck to the linoleum in a brown puddle. I looked into the sink. It was not something you wanted to approach without rubber gloves.

After searching in vain for cleaning materials, I took a walk around the neighborhood and found a little store where I purchased some dish detergent and Ajax. By the time Gale came home, the sink and the floor were clean, the dishes were washed, and I had tossed out several stinking concoctions from the refrigerator. Gale couldn't believe it. Why in the world had I wasted my first afternoon in Monterey, the most beautiful place on Planet Earth, *cleaning a kitchen?*

Cleaning was not something Gale and her friends regarded highly. Neither was having a job. Other than David and Ruben Ramir (nee Ramirez), two flamenco-guitar-playing brothers whose father op-erated a construction company, and who lived rent-free in one of the upscale apartment buildings their dad owned, just about everyone else I met that summer was on welfare—and proud of it. It was, they were quick to say, their way of sticking it to the government: CIA goons who installed dictatorships in third-world countries and kept Americans from the real truths of what was going on out there.

The only newspapers anyone ever read were underground tabloids, and those infrequently. Gale herself was bitter about working the fifteen well-paid hours a week that she did since it took time away from her painting. Framed water colors of tarot figures and mermaids covered the walls of her tiny dining room. Her watercolors, glowing inside heavily carved second-hand frames, were like fairytale illustrations, much more inviting to me than Judith's oil paintings.

Judith was sixty-five, maybe seventy. Matriarch of Monterey's enclave of latter-day hippies, she was fond of heavy eye make-up and brightly patterned scarves from which hung hanks of red-dyed hair. Judith liked to talk about her travels in Spain and Mexico—she had little use for America—as she drank wine paid for by either Gale or me. She claimed she was a Gypsy. The truth is, she looked like a bag lady who wore too much mascara. But she was adamant about the fact that she, her children, and her grandchildren came from true Gypsy Stock, which meant that the *duende* lived in their blood.

The third bedroom in Gale's house, the one overlooking the front yard, was Judith's painting studio. Gale rented it to her for a nominal fee. The oil paintings Judith created in there were so dark that any subject matter was indiscernible, but like the rest of her friends, Gale was convinced that Judith was that most esteemed of human beings: a True Artist.

But then, everyone I met that summer was an artist. In addition to playing the guitar, Ruben was a photographer. Or at least that's what everyone insisted; I'm not sure *Ruben* ever did. He was a mild-mannered young man whose sorrowful expression reminded me of Junior, the scrawny feline we adopted who was cuffed around by Kitty, Gale's big black house cat. Ruben was in love with Gale before she broke up with him to be with his brother, David. I don't remember who was older, Ruben or David, but I recall that David outshone Ruben in just about everything. David sang, painted, and wrote poetry. Unlike his stocky brother, he was slender and very good-looking. I liked David, just as I liked Ruben, but I was not enamored of him. My sister adored him. David Ramir was her ideal man and remains so to this day, despite any number of schoolgirl crushes since then on counselors, professors, and psychiatrists.

Ruben and David had real musical talent, unlike Patti. Patti was thirty-three and had a thirteen-year-old daughter she sometimes brought along with her when she came in from Big Sur to crash at our house for two or three or five days. Patti had a tangle of tawny hair, a nose ring, and a psyche scrubbed clean of any moral scruples. She looked like a lioness, and she was—but a lioness whose wealthy father was always ready to provide a fat check, as was her ex-husband, who was rich from dealing cocaine. Patti took what she wanted, when she wanted, from both. She would have bristled if you suggested she was anything but a free spirit. She painted splotched, ugly canvases and wrote what she called transcendental poems that she'd read out loud, swaying back and forth: *Black. Black. Black. Now wool, now wool. Mother of pearl eyes in lambs. I am drowning in black. I am drowning in lambs.*

There were other artists. There was Benny, twenty-seven, who rented a room from an elderly couple and played the bongo drums when he wasn't wandering the streets of Monterey with a large boom box blaring reggae. There was Rainbow, a hefty brunette who did psychic healing (fifty percent off on Tuesdays) and belly-danced. A variety of characters wove in and out of our days and nights that summer.

And then there was me. I had brought a suitcase full of freshly washed jeans, T-shirts, and blouses with me, ironed and folded in the basement of 206 South Raynor Avenue, the address I had lived my entire life except for sharing an apartment with Claire during her last year of law school at Indiana University. I hardly touched those clothes; Gale lent me skirts bought at the thrift shop and tie-dyed dresses much more fitting to *her* social gatherings. Friends drifted over at night and jammed in the backyard. One night, we had a bonfire as people drank wine, danced to guitars, and cried, "*Ole, ole!*"

Daniel, a charming folksinger and song writer around forty who I found out later accepted money from Judith for the favor of sleeping with her, leaned over to me that evening as I stood by the fire. "Something is beginning to bloom in you," he told me, looking into my eyes. "You're different than when you first came here." He told me he wanted to paint me for the way my long blond hair looked against the flames. I was flattered, but I knew Daniel grew effusive when he was drinking. The only difference between me that evening and when I stepped off the plane was the fact I was currently barefoot and clad in a long gauze shift.

If youth is wasted on the young, then beauty is wasted on the lonely. I was very lonely that summer, and Monterey was very beautiful. I loved to walk down to the pier in the evenings and watch the seals clamber and bark. Starfish clung to rocks lapped by salt water as pelicans glided and dipped above the bay. Sometimes as the sun set, sky and water were a pure, lambent lavender. I've never seen light or color like that since then. A few afternoons, I walked past the cluster of motels and restaurants built on the coastal curve where the bay widened and became ocean. Pink flowers blazed out of ledges leading like rough steps toward water. The ocean was more awesome than the bay, glittering and gargantuan, a great rolling god. I understood why the Greeks worshipped Poseidon.

I felt guilty that Monterey's beauty wasn't enough to make me happy. Walking home early evenings from the Caribbean Motel, where I worked as a maid, I'd climb on a rock overlooking the bay. *Look at this*, I'd tell myself fiercely, *you're so lucky!* I didn't feel lucky. I felt lost and homesick. I never knew once I got back to the house who was going to be there. I paid half the rent, but it was no more my house than Gale's friends were my friends. The one place that was mine was my bedroom, where I wrote in a spiral-bound journal and occasionally tried to compose poems. Gale was always after me to share my work. She couldn't understand why I didn't want to, or why I got annoyed because she insisted on introducing me as "my baby sister, the poet."

For all that she was an artist, Gale had little use for solitude; it was as if she were making up for lost time. She had never been popular in school and despised our home town. Joliet, Gale said, was the cultural nadir of the world, a place where people did nothing but drink beer and watch TV. Gale moved to Denver after college, spent some time in New Mexico, and eventually settled in Monterey. And there my sister blossomed. She never looked prettier to me than she did that summer. Tall and very slender, Gale favored long skirts and gauzy pastel dresses that suited her perfectly. She'd spritz her baby-fine hair with water to make it fuller, then fasten a flower in it. She had a proper California accent (she said *Kothy*, not *Kaaathy*) and a horror of anything Midwestern.

Among her bohemian friends, Gale luxuriated in at last being the center of attention. One evening she made us sit cross-legged on the floor of our candle-lit living room and hold pocket mirrors as she read Rilke's sonnet about mirrors:

Spendthrift! Still giving yourself away to the empty ballroom
when the dark dawn comes, as wide as the forests,
and the chandelier goes, like a sixteen-point stag
through your impossible gateway . . .

She liked doing stuff like that. And the *artistes* who dropped in were happy to put up with poetry—as long as they could drink her wine.

Not everyone was a hanger-on. There was Casey, who visited from Big Sur. Casey had been friends with Neil Cassady and Jack Kerouac. He had a grin craggy enough for romance novels and was one of the wittiest men I'd ever met. Like a lot of young women, I imagine, I was deeply infatuated with Casey within minutes of meeting him. And there was Pearl, a sweetheart of a woman, perhaps in her late fifties. That summer, Gale and I attended a dinner party hosted by Pearl and her husband, Ray, a Sicilian fisherman whose muscular forearms were nearly black from sun. We feasted on fresh scallops and squid as Ray urged us in a thickly accented voice to *have mora, have mora!*

Gale was gifted in pottery as well as painting. Hand-thrown bowls and vases were scattered throughout her house. Every morning I drank from a mug whose handle was a coyly arching gargoyle. I savored that cup as much as my sister's freshly ground coffee before heading off to the Caribbean Motel for a day of cleaning.

That's what I did that summer—cleaned motel rooms. It was important to me to pay half the expenses, but other than waitressing, there were few jobs to be had within walking distance of where we lived. I was shy; the very idea of waitressing terrified me. So along with a stream of small, efficient Filipino women, I cleaned motel rooms. My boss, the owner of the motel, was a woman by the name of Irene Delgado. I did not want to cross Irene. She had three daughters, all of them, frankly, swarthy, fat and ill-suited for the spandex tank tops and designer jeans they favored, along with all the expensive jewelry that could fit on their fingers and arms. The daughters shared a suite, which for some reason it was always my job to clean. I could not help feeling like Cinderella before the magic materialized. The Filipino ladies ignored me, chattering among themselves and probably wondering if that tall, blond girl was a little backward. The only maid slower than me was James.

To this day, I don't know if James had a screw loose, or if possibly he was a saint. Nothing annoyed or angered him. He had a gentle face and long hair pulled back in a ponytail. If James saw a plant that needed water, even if it was on someone else's porch, he'd find a way to give it a drink. He spent his free time tacking up hand-written flyers urging people to give up their automobiles and instead ride in "attractive carriages" powered by vegetable fuel. I sometimes fumed to James over the endless sheet-changing and sink cleaning and vacuuming that comprised our afternoons. I wanted *him* to be resentful too, but he never was. The only time James ever came close to disagreeing with me was when I noted with bitterness one evening, after we had cleaned nearly the entire third floor of the motel, that the only way to be free was to be rich. "Oh, no," James assured me benignly as he pushed the towel cart towards the storage room. "You read and write poetry, don't you? You'll always be free."

I left Monterey in October. I needed to do so in order to redeem my airline ticket, but that wasn't the reason I left. I was homesick. I missed my family, and I missed the Midwest: the green grass, the maple and oak trees that turned golden and red in autumn, the marigolds that bloomed damp and spicy by Mom's statue of St. Francis in the backyard. Gale didn't understand. She had never been able to divine a glint of grace in her hometown or, for that matter, her childhood. It was as if we grew up in two different families.

David Ramir, Gale's ideal man and soul mate, hosted a party for me the night before I left. He and his brother played flamenco as people made toasts with pinot noir. I wore a black skirt and a rhinestone-studded vest. My hair was wild from my not having combed it very carefully for a while. Patti, the lioness, did an interpretive dance, which was far better than either her poetry or her painting. David read a poem he had written for me called "Platinum Rose." Even Judith, whom I sensed had never liked me, thawed into cordiality that final evening. Later, we drank cognac as we listened to Eric Satie's *Gymnopedies* and *Gnossiennes*. I had never heard these piano compositions before. I knew I would never forget them, these pieces that sounded like haiku put to music. I wondered that night if maybe I should forget about my return ticket and stay in Monterey.

―――――――――――――――

How ironic that it wasn't until after Gale came home a year later, shocked into silence from her first and most devastating bout with schizophrenia, that closeness finally began to blossom between us. It hadn't been there the summer I lived with her. Gale was as much a stranger to me then as her friends were. She enjoyed showing me off as her baby sister, but we never really talked or confided in each other. I remember once getting into her beat up Volkswagen (you had to climb over the driver's seat to get into the passenger's because the passenger door wouldn't open) and leaning by mistake on the gear shift.

"Jesus *fuck*, Francine! I need this car for my job. Be careful!" I stared straight ahead of me as she drove, my lips shaking. When Gale apologized awkwardly a few minutes later, I said it was fine, but I wanted to bawl: me, the clumsy, inadequate younger sister. But when Gale came back to Joliet, I was the older sister.

Later, when Gale grew well enough to take graduate classes at the College of St. Francis and begin student teaching, we were simply friends. I was then living on Wells Street in Old Town; Gale visited me on weekends. We went to art fairs and galleries together. I still have books she gave to me in thanks for my hospitality, and sometimes for no reason at all: marvelous collections by Sylvia Plath, and Baudelaire, and Rilke.

Gale managed to move away from Joliet and rent a small apartment in Hyde Park, but the strain of living alone and working a full time job proved too great. After a relapse and time spent in a grim institution located in one of the poorest areas of Illinois, my sister moved into a group house on the north side of Chicago. The neighborhood was dicey, but the apartment itself was sunny and clean. Gale had roommates, compassionate counselors, and a fat Persian cat who was spoiled by all the residents. She seemed finally to have achieved some balance and joy in her life when she was struck by a speeding car just blocks from her home.

After months in the hospital, my sister learned to walk again with the aid of a cane. She returned to the group house where she had been living, but it was clear they could not accommodate someone with her physical disabilities. That's when Gale moved into Greenwood Care, a state-run facility in Evanston, Illinois, just north of Chicago. All told, she has been in and out of more hospitals and institutions than most people would care to imagine. She has endured the terror and iso-lation that accompanies mental illness and immeasurable smaller losses: she can't scramble eggs in her own kitchen, or light a candle in her room, or come home to her own pet curled up on the chair. Her address is a nursing home for the mentally ill, and her living room is shared by an entire floor of residents, most of whom are nowhere near her intel-ligence level.

Two things have remained constant in Gale's life: our friend-ship, and her rhapsodic memories of life in Monterey. How Gale loves to reminisce about Casey, and Judith, and the good times we had that summer I lived with her. How beautiful California was, and how happy she had been! Every Christmas, Gale sends brag letters to people she knew more than twenty-five years ago, people who may or may not still be living in Monterey, telling them about her successful life and career:

Merry Christmas! Happy Chanukah! Joyous Winter Solstice!

It has been a busy and productive year for me as a writer and artist! I completed my narrative poetry manuscript SACRED SANCTITY OF THE SEXUALITY OF SOULMATES—the love story of two soul mates spanning from the Beginning of Time until the Present, written in lyric verse, assonance, and extensive and difficult Rhyme . . . I am still studying toward a Divinity Degree at the Carl Jung Institute and had three Art Exhibits this

year . . . I am studying Tarot and in great demand as a reader . . .As always,
I am publishing my line drawings in poetry journals, and I hope to have at
least two more chapbooks of poetry published soon . . .Happy Holidays!
Please write! Sending tons of love!

She tells me gleefully how jealous they must be of her. I don't know how many of Gale's former friends have ever written back. I know that for a while, David returned her letters unopened.

Although it seems they arrived at a kind of truce. About five years after Gale moved into Greenwood, David wrote Gale, telling her about his divorce, the death of his father, and his continued interest in painting. From the way Gale described it, his letter sounded a little sad and not at all unkind. David Ramir was not a cruel man. I still have the thin packet of letters he wrote me after I moved back to Joliet. *After you left to return to Joliet we exchanged a few letters. But you stopped writing—and I know it was because of my involvement with Gale. I tried to explain, in a diplomatic way, that I loved Gale but I was not in love . . . I believe you must have known it was you who I was in love with.*

How strange to consider this confession more than two decades later. Where was I when I first read that letter? How did I respond? I don't remember. Nor have I ever been tempted to step back, in my imagination, into that golden, lonely summer when I was twenty-two and had long blond hair and two flamenco playing brothers infatuated with me. I am wary of nostalgia. To write about the past, to push oneself to remember, like a particular shade of blue, the tone of a lost afternoon, to connect that afternoon with other lost afternoons and conversations, to strive to find meaning, or at least pattern, in one's life by examining the past—that I can do. But to relive it just for the supposed pleasure of reliving it? I believe that's dangerous.

I think of David's mother. She was a notorious beauty in her twenties. A West Coast artist who was very sought-after at the time asked if he could paint her portrait. It hung above the mantle of the Ramirez home when David and Ruben were growing up. It continued to hang there as the two brothers grew older. Carmelita Ramirez, in her sixties, with dyed black hair and eyes that welled too easily, would drink brandy in the evening and cry in front of it. "Wasn't I beautiful?" she would ask her husband, as she sipped a generous snifter of brandy. Gale told me that story the summer I lived with her.

In 2001, I moved from Chicago to Kansas to get a Masters in English. From Kansas, I moved to Minneapolis to work towards an MFA at the University of Minnesota. I visited Gale in January of my second year at the U of M. I hadn't seen her for nearly four years. We talked on the phone every week, but I worried about her. I was the only sister who was truly close with Gale. I spent three days in Evanston over Christmas break. A large shopping bag was waiting for me at the front desk of the Ramada Inn. In it were about five pounds worth of single-spaced typed poems stapled into various volumes with illustrated covers; two dresses from a used clothing store; and an effusive hand-written letter from Gale greeting her beloved sister and informing me she was waiting for me at the Café Espresso, one block south of Greenwood Care.

When I met Gale at her old hangout, it was as if no time had passed. She seemed exactly the same, with her coffee-stained dress and her three or four heavy silver and turquoise necklaces, her big can of loose tobacco, her tarot cards. She was no longer slender, due partly to the medication she took, which bloats the body. But she still had her beautiful jade-green eyes and a coy smile, as if she were belle of the ball. She flirted with children and introduced me to every customer she possibly could ("Andy? Andy! I want you to meet my baby sister! Andy's a Buddhist. He's very smart!"). She insisted on calling me *darling* and giving me career advice in a voice that carried across the room as she blew her nose loudly into napkins (she had a bad cold), then stuffed them in her pockets.

We went out to dinner that evening. Over a meal of oysters Rockefeller, pan-fried trout, and the one glass of white wine I let her order, it did not take Gale long to return to her favorite subject, Monterey. Once again, I heard about Judith, about Casey, about David. "Poor David! I think he's been jealous for years of my artistic success.

He was never very talented. But he was sure *handsome*, wasn't he? I even thought about lending him to you for a night that summer you came out. Wasn't that a wonderful summer?"

It was cold and icy walking back from the restaurant to Greenwood. Even with her cane, Gale didn't dare to let go of my arm. We walked slowly, for fear of her slipping. I noticed as we passed under a streetlight that her lips were moving ever so slightly. Every once in a while she smiled, as if to acknowledge a compliment.

Oh Gale, I thought, clutching her hand tight. I remembered taking walks with her in Joliet twenty years earlier and wondering if she knew I was there, beside her. It was easy to forget how vulnerable she still was. Gale always *sounded* cheerful when we talked on the phone. She enjoyed telling me in great detail about the poetry she was writing, and the books she was reading, and the excellent advice she was dispensing to various residents (Gale loved to give advice). Often, it was hard for me to finish a sentence. I'd hold the phone away from my ear as she chattered on and on.

But sometimes we had wonderful conversations, ones during which we laughed and joked as any two sisters might. We both loved poetry and literature, and Gale's knowledge of art and psychology was considerable. Her interpretations of my dreams were witty and usually spot on. And her respect for the choices I'd made never failed to touch me. I was her only unmarried sister, and I was definitely in the lowest financial bracket. But Gale would remind me how much Planet Earth needed poets, how *important* my role was. She ended nearly every one of our conversations by sending love to Marc—"my favorite brother-in-law!"—and "the babes," my two cats.

I visited Gale at Greenwood the last day of my trip. The windowless lobby smelled of stale cigarette smoke and cleaning fluid. While I waited for my sister to come down from her room on the sixth floor, residents shuffled past me in various states of dress, some muttering, some staring straight ahead. One woman, about fifty, came up to me and informed me that her boyfriend wanted to buttfuck her because she was a dirty prostitute. "Now Nancy, we don't talk that way 'round here," said the receptionist, a large black woman who had given me a warm smile when I first came in. Nancy began to protest but soon gave in to the receptionist's soothing but firm admonishments. The receptionist, whose name was Mary, turned to me. "I'm sure glad you came by to see Gale. She gets real lonely."

Gale told me how much my visit meant to her as we sat on her bed in the dorm-like room she shared with another resident. "I wish you still lived in Chicago! We could have coffee every Saturday. I could introduce you to my friends at the Unitarian Church. It's my social center now. Everyone knows me!" We were looking at water colors she had spread across the bed: paintings of nymphs and goddesses, the same fairytale creatures she liked to draw when she was a child. She wanted to give me one as a going away present.

"Look, Gale," I said, holding up a large painting of an angel, "her wings are full of tears. They look like they're crying."

Gale glanced at the angel. "Oh, no, that's just the way I put in the shadows. Those aren't tears. I'm going to go have a cigarette in the day room, darling. Choose whichever painting you like! I'll be back in five minutes."

A photograph of a portrait of David, painted by Judith, was pinned on the wall behind me. For once, Judith had not used oils so dark that you couldn't make out anything. David did indeed look very handsome, a soulful Spanish poet. There were other photographs pinned up there as well, all from Monterey, all from many years ago. As I waited for Gale to return, a voice came on the loudspeaker announcing, amid static, something about meds. Two residents in the hall quarreled about a cookie.

Gale's room was small. She and her roommate each had a narrow bed, a chest of drawers, and one shelf. I sat on her bed at Greenwood Care that afternoon surrounded by painted mermaids and goddesses, staring at the stiff watercolor I was holding: an emotionless angel. She had my sister's face, and great, weeping wings.

❄Part Four❄

Blooming Late

BLOOMING LATE

My mother was not a poet, but metaphors came naturally to her. To this day when I see an August sky scattered with broken clouds at dusk, I imagine they are little lambs going home to sleep. She told me that once at bedtime. She used to say the cottonwood tree on Willow Avenue, the one Claire and I could see glittering from our bedroom window, held real gold. She called the white fluff of seeds from that tree, the stuff that drifted into soft banks throughout our neighborhood, "summer snow." I remember helping my mother prepare dinner one afternoon when I was eighteen and had just finished my first year at Joliet Junior College. Vegetables spilled across the kitchen table: red and yellow peppers, carrots, leaf lettuce wet and glistening. "Look, Frannie," my mother exclaimed, "it's October!"

Mom gave birth to me when she was forty. I believe our age difference was one of the reasons we got along so well. There were none of the rivalries that so often occur between a mother and daughter separated by twenty rather than forty years. "Your mother looks like a *grandma*," Kathy Henderson said to me once when we were playing. I knew that Kathy, an engaging child several years younger than me, was not trying to insult me. Mom had a comfortable lap and knotted blue veins that were hidden only when she wore support stockings. I hated those ugly bulging veins, but they never seemed to bother *her* as she watered flowers in the backyard in shorts and sandals or knelt beside day lilies with shears and a spade, weeding, pruning, lifting stones that revealed living mosaics of insects. I'd screech and run away while my mother calmly continued to garden.

Two good dresses hung in my mother's closet, one paisley, the other shell-pink. The make-up in the top drawer of her dresser—little red boxes of solid mascara, elaborate tubes of lipstick—was years old. She looked nothing like Kathy's mother, who could not have been more than twenty-seven or twenty-eight. Mrs. Henderson wore glamorous sunglasses, and her nails were long and polished. My mother's hands were large and freckled, with baggy knuckles. They were hands accustomed to cutting up whole chickens and upholstering the fabric on the seats of dining room chairs. The nails were not polished.

My kindergarten picture.

The year I turned five, I was lucky enough to have my mother to myself weekday mornings. My older sisters were in school and my father either at the piano store or out on tuning jobs. In the afternoon, I attended kindergarten at Sheridan Grammar School—the class of 1964—but Mom never made me go if I didn't want to. *Mama*, I called her then. We'd go shopping at Jewel, a small grocery store on Jefferson Street just blocks from our house. Next, Mom would stop at a bakery located in the same plaza, then we'd visit Ben Franklin's, a store that had everything important in the world, from doll clothing to kaleidoscopes. This time spent alone with my mother bonded me deeply to her. Except for Lenore, the oldest, I was the only daughter who got to have it.

Our orange tomcat, Pumpkin, died that fall. I remember huddling in the big chair in the living room, sobbing for our cat who was now in Heaven. Based on the smattering of Catholicism I'd absorbed, I imagined Pumpkin ascending to the sky like the Virgin Mary, floating first above telephone poles, then rooftops, then the three cottonwood trees in our neighborhood, surely the tallest trees in the world. Pumpkin's death opened the door to the possibility of other, more terrible deaths. More than once, I crept into my parents' bedroom at night to ask my mother if she, too, was going to die. My mother doubtless calmed me, but I don't know if she ever said *no*. She'd lost her own mother when she was only seven.

My grandmother, a long-necked girl of Austrian descent, died after what was apparently a botched hysterectomy. Mom never spoke much about her mother for the simple reason that she remembered so little about her, but I always had the impression her barely remembered presence was like an heirloom, something so precious it should be handled only occasionally. I've seen only one picture of my grandmother, whose name was Florence Potch Kelly, and who was seventeen years younger than my grandfather. It's an oval-shaped photograph in which she stands in a floor-length skirt and a fitted blouse buttoned nearly to her chin. She is slender as a ballerina, with a dark pompadour and lovely, grave eyes. Florence reminds me of the rosebud-bordered china she inherited from her own mother, impossibly light plates and cups that lay wrapped in layers of tissue in the middle drawers of my Aunt Margie's buffet.

Florence's wake was held in the Kelly house and was open casket. Mom told me about it one evening as we sat in the kitchen after dinner, each of us sipping a glass of wine. "I looked at the lady in the coffin and I thought, this *can't* be my mother. My mother knows how much I miss her—she's coming back. I remember a woman in a great big hat with a veil took hold of me and insisted I kiss my dear mother good-bye. I'm sure she meant well, but I was so frightened. How I struggled to get away from that woman! I don't know what I would have done if Papa hadn't seen what was happening."

Papa told his youngest daughter she did not have to kiss her mother if she was afraid, but he knew better than to lie to her about her mama returning. One of my favorite photographs of my mother was taken about a year after her mother died. She and my Aunt Ginny stand beside a pony, scowling. I know my mother, at least, was scowling. With her bobbed hair and her sailor suit, she is adorable, but her eyes dare you to lie to her. Papa would not have risked losing his child's trust by telling her fairytales about death.

Mom always said their mother's death was hardest on Marjorie. I don't doubt her, but it was typical of my mother to downplay her own loss. Her childhood stories are happy. Joliet was a steel town, but people still raised chickens in their backyards and tended vegetable gardens. Sometimes men looking to exchange labor for a meal knocked at the back door of the Kelly house. "We always gave them a sandwich and an apple, whatever we had," Mom told me. "Papa would have been mad if we didn't."

Papa, a guard at Stateville Penitentiary, could not afford to send Mom to the town's Catholic college as he had Marjorie, even though Helen Kelly was in the top ten of her class at Joliet Township and a winning debate team member. Instead, my mother attended Joliet Junior College, then located at the high school, and went from there to a secretarial school in Chicago. If she couldn't be a lawyer, Mom told me, she intended to enter the business world the only way possible: as a secretary. "But I had no intentions of *staying* a secretary. I was too ambitious."

Looking at the photographs I have of my mother, I doubt if the word "ambitious" would come to mind. When she was in her twenties, she was gorgeous, with Hollywood legs and a smile as dazzling as it was sweet. In one picture she stands against Lake Michigan, dark hair blowing across her face, as my dad snaps the photo. They have driven to Chicago to spend the day, this lovely young woman and handsome ex-soldier with blue eyes and thick blond hair. She's wearing a dark skirt with a wide patent leather belt that emphasizes her slen-der waist; her strapped

Helen and Arthur, May 1947.

high heels are sexy and impractical. In a later picture, she sits on a toy-cluttered couch with two toddlers lolling against her and a baby—Myra, the third oldest—on her lap. There are pictures of her holding cats and hugging dogs, watering ferns in a pink flannel robe striped with sun from venetian blinds.

But flowers and sunny rooms are only half my mother's story. She helped my father manage a piano store and was far better at the financial end of it than he was. She saw to it that all six of her daughters learned how to swim and type, drive a car, and cook a decent meal. Claire stammered in grammar school; Mom worked with her in the kitchen after supper every evening, making her read aloud and recite tongue twisters. It might not have been correct, but it was the only way Mom knew how to help. Katherine was passionate about the theater; my mother coached her for every school audition and attended all her plays. At the age of fifty-six, my mother began selling furniture at Montgomery Ward. She hadn't worked full time outside the home in almost three decades, but she was the furniture department's top salesperson that year—and every year after until she re-tired.

I'm not being falsely modest when I say I am not the woman my mother was, but I do have her dogged determination to do my best. That may be good for a writer, but it's an inconvenient way to live. Whether I'm working at a miserable part-time job or composing a letter to the editor of a newspaper, I *can't* do a sloppy job. I don't know how I would have been as a mother. I knew even as a child that having children would not be right for me. I'm not sure *how* I knew; I loved playing with my baby dolls and worried about hurting the feelings of my stuffed animals. But I never longed for my own babies.

This is something I felt guilty about for years, yet Mom understood my feelings. She never believed a woman had to have babies to be fulfilled. She even admitted that if she weren't convinced at the time it was a sin, she would have welcomed birth control. In the space of nine years, and at a time when there were no Pampers, no microwaves, and no day care, my mother had six daughters and two miscarriages—both, sadly, boys. Little wonder that after Claire's birth, which had been particularly difficult, she suffered depression. "My sisters were wonderful," Mom told me. "Ginny, Lucille. Both of them did what they could. But I don't know what I would have done that summer without Margie."

By then, Mom was thirty-eight years old and a mother of five. She tried to ignore her post-partum depression. She had four little girls to take care of besides the baby, meals to prepare, laundry. By summer, she couldn't do it. Maybe it was Dad who persuaded her to see a doctor. I'll never know what secrets she unburdened to that psychiatrist. She told me that as exhausted as she was, she could not sleep; she had an obsession to keep moving her legs, rubbing them against each other in bed. Marjorie came over nearly every day. A schoolteacher at Hufford Junior High, my aunt had summers off. Marjorie cooked and cleaned, played games with Lenore, Katherine, Myra and Gale, and rocked the baby. She saved my mother's life.

When Pearl Harbor was attacked, Mom was twenty-four and working as an executive's assistant at an ad agency in Chicago. She quit her job and joined the Women's Marine Corps. This was something that embarrassed me as a child, like the knotted veins on her legs. Why would a woman join the Marines? What *good* did they do anyway? I'm sure part of her reason for enlisting must have been a yen for adventure and a chance to travel, but she also sincerely wanted to do something for her country. Mom was stationed at Camp LaJeune, in North Carolina. She kept her medals in an ivory-colored box that sat in the top drawer of her dresser. When I was little, she'd let me examine its contents—curious pins with bits of striped ribbon, not nearly as interesting as her costume jewelry.

I never asked what the medals were for. There were so many questions I never asked. The only two things I know for sure about my mother's Marine Corps years is that she became a sergeant and that one of her jobs was to review and edit war films. Years later, when she was in her seventies, my mother declared one night out of the blue that she wished she had never seen some of those films. "It wasn't right, the things they made a young woman watch," she said. Those words were like a jolt of lightning on the horizon of a quiet evening. She never elaborated.

My parents married not long after my dad returned to Joliet from Honolulu, where he was stationed during the war. "I saw your

Helen Kelly with three Marine Corps pals. My mother is far right.

mother on the steps of St. Patrick's church," Dad told me and my sisters, "and I said to myself, 'That's the girl I'm going to spend the rest of my life with. No ifs ands or buts!'" My father, a Swedish Baptist who kept a wide girth from Catholic relics and scapulars, was happy to participate in a Novena that evening. He was rewarded by Helen Kelly accepting his invitation to have a drink at the Hotel Louis Joliet. They walked there, since Arthur Tolf didn't own a car.

Their marriage wasn't perfect. There were financial crises. My mother could be moody, and when she was, it was as if a thick gray cloud sat in every room of our house. Dad went through a god-awful Fundamentalist phase during which Jimmy Swaggart praised the Lord from our television set. But my parents' love for each other was deeper than any anxiety caused by money trouble, or mood swings, or even religious fever. Dad adored Mom. "Isn't your mother a wonderful cook?" he'd say, whether Mom made beef stew (which actually was delicious) or shriveled pork chops with canned tomatoes. He always said Mom was smarter than he was. "You girls get your brains from your mother, not me." As for Mom, I remember her greeting Dad at the door with endearments she made up: "Arter, the light of my life, the joy of my days!" She was as unself-conscious about saying things like that as she was about cheerfully belting out "Mac the Knife" while chopping potatoes.

I said that my mother wasn't a poet, but that's not true. She used to write light verse; she'd compose poems for our birthdays and other occasions. She tried to draw, too. I found a sketchbook of hers while going through the drawers of a cabinet some days after her funeral. The sketches were not very good: crude, almost child-like, but I could tell it was Wilmington Lake, where we used to have Sunday picnics and go swimming. There was a newspaper clipping in the same drawer, a letter to the editor of the *Joliet Herald News* from Helen Tolf in which she praised the lovely greenhouses and gardens of Pilcher Park. Dad—no doubt it was Dad, proud of every one of Mom's accomplishments—had laminated the clipping, darkened to brown now beneath its coat of plastic.

Several weeks after Mom's death, when September days still held late summer luxuriance, I began a poetry writing class at Chicago's

Newberry Library. I was thirty-nine. I had an almost physical ache to write, although I wasn't sure what I wanted or needed to say. I started to read poetry seriously as well. I had so much catching up to do. As our class neared its end, my instructor asked me if I would care to join his own poetry group. I said yes with pleasure; poetry had quietly become an indispensable part of my life.

My mother's death caused that shift in me, although I don't know why or how. I had composed poems when I was a child; meter and rhyme came naturally to me. Teachers loved my verses, which were filled with adjectives like "dappled" and "lacey." I liked playing with words, but I knew what I wrote wasn't *poetry*. Poetry was the inexplicable sadness I felt when my family was driving home from somewhere at dusk and I could see telephone wires growing crisp and black against a yellow sky. It was my friend Adrienne's face one afternoon when she was daydreaming in class—goofy, unimaginative Adrienne!—and that moment looked gravely beautiful.

I wrote what I'd call my first real poem when I was nineteen: "Marigolds in November." It contained some archaic language, but a breath of those spicy-scented flowers lived in my lines. After I finished, I felt excited and happy and serious all at once. I showed the poem to my mother that evening. She came into my bedroom after she read it.

"Frannie, your poem is beautiful. Just beautiful."

How my heart leapt to hear that. "You really like it, Mom?"

"Oh, honey, I do. You make me see those marigolds. 'A hundred suns that tremble in the cold / and shake their spangled globes of ruffled gold.' You have a real gift with language!"

I continued writing poetry throughout my college years, the last two of which were spent at Joliet's College of St. Francis, the Catholic school that Mom could not afford to attend. Every few weeks, I'd give Mom two or three poems to read at night as she sat in her chair in the bedroom talking with Dad, already lounging in bed, leafing through *U.S. News* and listening to the radio. Mom read my work as if it were a privilege, not a favor. She made me feel as if my poems about our hollyhocks and one-eared tomcat, Beauregard, were important and wonderful.

We read poetry together too: Robert Frost, e.e. cummings, William Butler Yeats. Mom understood them better than I did: *An aged man is but a paltry thing, / A tattered coat upon a stick, unless / Soul clap its hands and sing, and louder sing / For every tatter in its mortal dress.* I wasn't moved by those words until my mother read "Sailing to Byzantium" out loud. Then I heard their faith and poignancy. I continued to write poetry for a while after I graduated, but less and less regularly. If Mom was disappointed I didn't stick to my writing, she never said so. She always said I was the one daughter she didn't worry about—which is funny, because I'd done nothing to make her particularly proud. I graduated with honors from college, but after that I drifted. I spent eight months in Bloomington, Indiana, during Claire's third year of law school, then five months in Monterey, living with Gale. After returning home, I worked briefly in Joliet, then moved to Chicago when I was twenty-four.

Eventually, I became a legal secretary. Mom used to tell people I was a paralegal; I wasn't. It has occurred to me that I might have been naïve about Mom's seemingly uncomplicated feelings for me. At the age of thirty-nine, the year my mother died, I was a secretary, the position she said would never have satisfied her. I had no marriage, no children, and, apparently, no ambition.

Mom wrote me a letter about my poetry once when I was in my late twenties and for a few sweet, surprising months started writing again. I had sent her a few new poems. She wrote me they were alive, made her think and feel. *Don't stop writing* is what the letter begs, although she never says that. It's a letter I will always keep. But it is a later note, a note my mother sent me along with what must have been a modest check, just five months before she died, that made my throat tighten when I re-read it:

Dearest Frannie,
A little gift for you to enjoy as you will. All is well. Remember Robert Browning's "Pippa's Song":

> *The year's at the spring,*
> *And day's at the morn;*

Morning's at seven;
The hillside's dew-pearled;
The lark's on the wing;
The snail's on the thorn;
God's in His heaven—
All's right with the world!

Our days of spring are arriving.
With love, Mother

She must have written that at her dining room desk, placed under the window that overlooks the backyard, then Willow Avenue. Sitting there, I could see what I believed as a child to be the tallest tree in the world, a cottonwood that held real gold. I think of my mother at the age of seventy-nine, husband and dearest sister gone, recording those lines of Browning for me that April morning. No hesitation in her distinct, slightly angular script.

Friends say I idealize her. Well, of course I do. I don't know how *not* to idealize the woman who taught me what beauty was and how to love it, the only adult throughout my childhood and teenage years who consistently made me feel important and validated. I idealize my mother the way Claire idealizes Dad and Gale, Margie. She represents unconditional love to me. Yet how I wanted to please her!

I remember sitting on a chair at the kitchen table, my legs dangling above the speckled linoleum, watching my mother prepare dinner. She opened a can of peaches, poured the juice into a glass, and set it down in front of me. "Drink this up, Yipper," she said, using her pet name for me. "It's a treat." I didn't like the juice; it was too thick and too sweet. But even at five, I could not disappoint my mother. I drank the whole glass, pretending it tasted delicious.

Am I as adept at denial as my mother was? She never admitted that Dad had the least sign of dementia. And I remember her telling us more than once about the beautiful smile her sister Lucille gave her as she lay on Margie's bed just hours before she passed away. "Such a happy, peaceful smile!" Mom would say. I found out later that Lucille hadn't even asked for Mom to be at her bedside. That was Marjorie's doing. No Kelly sister would have put it so starkly, but Mom and Lucille had been estranged for years. Who knows what really happened when my mother visited her older sister for the last time?

One thing is for sure: my mother would have walked into that bedroom without revealing a trace of guilt or nervousness. Her self-confidence was born of pure will, of what she needed to believe. She was the woman who could read books that demonized the mothers of schizophrenic children and insist with convincing sincerity that such criticism had no affect on her. But inside my mother was the trembling vulnerability that is inside all of us. I saw it exposed only once. I was in my late twenties and in Joliet for the weekend. Lenore and her husband had had another of their fights, which meant that Lenore had visited both Mom and Margie, telling her side of the quarrel and how cruel Bill had been. My mother had been through this many times before. She knew that two days from now, Lenore would have made up with Bill and forgotten her claims of abuse. But Katherine, who also was in Joliet for the weekend, had never forgiven Bill for how he treated Lenore before they were married. We were in the living room talking about it, Katherine and Mom and I. Our discussion became heated. The several glasses of wine each of us had drunk probably didn't help.

"Frankly, Mother, I don't know how you tolerate the man," Katherine said. "I know you say Bill's done favors for you and Dad. I don't care. Don't you remember the fights he and Lenore used to get into before they got married? I remember sitting on a table in West Park with Lenore. She was telling me the names Bill called her the night before. *Filthy* names. Then she put her head in my lap and just started to sob. I'll never forget that." Katherine, the former theater major, milked all the drama from these words that she could. They must have been salt in the wound to our mother, who, in fact, had vehemently opposed Lenore's and Bill's marriage.

"Katherine, Katherine, it's not—"

"No, I mean it! How can you be nice to him? After how he treated your own daughter?"

I remember what happened next as if through blurred glass. There are more words between Katherine and Mom, then I see my mother at the top of the landing with Katherine following her, reaching out to touch her, and I hear my mother crying, "Don't touch me! Don't touch me! You don't know, you have no idea." Who *was* this raw, wild, hurt woman?

My mother also happened to be, like me, very deeply a creature of habit. Her comforts may have been modest, but she was loath to give them up. When Claire and I were still best friends, her husband got transferred to the London branch of his law office. It was there, far from the rest of her family, that Claire suffered a miscarriage at seven months. I do not think I understood at the time how traumatic it must have been for Claire. She knew her baby was lifeless when doctors induced labor. Claire told our mother about it during a long-distance call. A few days later, Mom called me. "Your father and I have discussed this, Frannie," she said in a bright voice. "We want to give you the money for airfare to spend a week in London with Claire." I was stunned—and not in a good way. My mother *knew* how much I disliked traveling. I slept poorly away from home and (to put it bluntly) became miserably constipated.

I knew Mom's "gift" was her way of compensating for the fact that she could not bring herself to travel to London herself. She would have said this was because she could not leave Dad alone, but it would be another five years before he showed the least sign of dementia. Dad would have been fine. Mom simply hated and feared the idea of getting on a plane and being a guest in her daughter and son-in-law's house.

As for me, I was so reluctant to spend seven days overseas that for once, I did not immediately give in to my mother's wishes. "That's very generous of you, Mom," I said cautiously, "but I'm going to have to think it over. It's not that I wouldn't love to see Claire. But it's very busy at work. Let me get back to you."

My mother did not expect this, but managed to keep the brightness in her voice. "You do that, honey. I know Claire would love to see you. Think about it."

Marc was the one person who understood my reluctance to travel had nothing to do with how much I loved Claire. "You don't have to go, Frannie. You're thirty years old. You don't have to do what your mother tells you to do anymore. Why isn't your mother going to London?"

"Mom's never going to get in a plane and cross the ocean," I snapped, taking out my frustration on the one person who understood it. "I'll call Claire. I won't tell her about Mom's offer. I want to hear how she sounds, how she's coping."

I called Claire early the next morning. She was extremely happy to hear from me. We talked, we even laughed, and I thought to myself, *she's going to be all right. I don't have to do this.* I asked Claire if she could talk about the miscarriage. She did, bravely, but her voice broke when she began to describe the funeral service for "our little girl." I knew then that it was no longer a question of, "do I have to visit Claire?" Of course I had to visit her. Screw the fact that I wasn't going to sleep or shit for a week. I had to comfort my dear, broken-hearted sister.

Yet I can't bring myself to condemn Mom, who was then seventy, for not going to London herself. I can't think the less of her for not champing at the bit to babysit her grandchildren and tote them to school and lessons and sports games the way Margie did. My mother had raised one family. She was content to let her daughters raise theirs. This seemed like a perfectly reasonable position to me, but I'm not sure it did to my three sisters who had children.

Maybe if I, too, had had children, my feelings for my mother would have been very different. But I didn't. She was the mother who always *was* there for me, the woman who opened her home to a chain-smoking schizophrenic daughter for six years, the wife who cleaned her husband's soiled sheets and wiped his fingers with a wet cloth as tenderly as if he were a baby. She was the person who insisted, long after I had graduated from college and stopped writing, that I was a poet.

One Saturday morning after Dad had passed away, my mother and I sat in the kitchen drinking coffee. The day was colorless and cold. Somehow the kitchen's artificial light made it more, not less, depressing. The room was cluttered—indeed, every room was cluttered—with items Mom had picked up at garage sales. During the two or three years before Dad's health sharply declined, my parents browsed every Saturday among garage sales. ("I never knew there was so many garages in one town," my father once noted gloomily.)

The stove was slick with grime. My mother appeared preoccupied. She lit a Virginia Slim and turned on a small electric fan—another garage sale trophy—that was supposed to get rid of second hand smoke. "I was thinking, Frannie. I was thinking of writing some of my stories down. Memoirs, I guess you'd call them." She spoke almost shyly.

"That's a wonderful idea, Mom! You should do it. You have such good material."

I meant it. But sitting in that cheerless kitchen, I knew my mother was never going to write down any stories. It was the expression that passed like a cloud across her face when she spoke of doing just that. What was that expression? Sadness, bewilderment, defeat? I cannot name it, but I knew I was seeing the face behind my mother's willed self-confidence. That's the moment I committed myself to writing my mother's stories for her, although I had no idea how I was going to do this. Writing about real life seemed as difficult that day as it had when I was eleven and tried, unsuccessfully, to describe an afternoon at St. Patrick's Grammar School.

I titled the first really promising poem I wrote after completing the Newberry Library writing class and joining my instructor's poetry group, "My Mother in Summer." I felt deeply satisfied after finishing it, the way I felt after writing "Marigolds in November." And like that earnest nineteen-year-old, the thirty-nine-year-old woman I now was wanted to show her handiwork to her mother. *Look, Mama, I wrote you a poem!* I forgot, for a moment, that she was dead.

Having written seriously since her death in 1997, I now have three chapbooks and finally—finally!—a full-length book of poetry that I would love to share with my mother. I think she'd like my work although people sometimes say it's sad. "Why don't you write *happy* poems, Frannie?" Katherine once asked me in exasperation. I don't mean to write sad poems. I hope the core of me holds joy, not sorrow, but I can't help but be tempered by experience. I remember 206 South Raynor as a house filled with light, but I also remember the buckled ceilings, the increasingly ragged neighborhood. I see my mother placing lilacs in a bowl on the dining room table, and I see her bruised body on a hospital bed during my last visit with her, when she could barely drink water. I think Mom would understand how beauty, for me, is never without its rim of sadness, even though *she*—Tuesday's child—had the gift of delight.

I'm Thursday's child, the one who had far to go and got off to a late start. Didn't begin writing seriously until I was nearly forty, didn't come to terms with my father until more than ten years after he died, didn't realize how much *I'm* to blame for flawed relations with certain sisters until I began writing about them.

In the summer of 2005, Lenore and Bill, parents of five, suffered the loss of one of their sons. Brendan was twenty-two year old and took his own life. This tragedy dispersed any remaining bad feelings between me and my oldest sister. We talk sometimes, Lenore and me. She has a strong temper but a generous heart, one that has been tested by pain I do not think I could have borne. Lenore now counsels young men at Stateville's Youth Correctional Center, and she does it with humor and compassion. Before her son's death, I'm sure my oldest sister would have said her life's purpose was being a mother. She told me during a recent phone conversation that she now believes it's being with those young men, giving them time and attention they've never had.

Katherine has been a rock to me since our mother's death. She's the sister who tells me I'm beautiful, who gives me outlandish compliments I know are not true but enjoy hearing anyway. ("Frannie, I read this Lisel Mueller poet you're so crazy about. I don't see why. Your poetry is clearly so much better!") Throughout the course of her life, my second oldest sister has modeled, sold designer clothing, and bought women's clothing for a department store in Greenwich. She's currently—of all things—the director of Admissions to a prep school located near her and David's house in Connecticut. Katherine has put her acting talent to good use in every job she's ever had, but she is at last back on the real stage where she belongs. She's active in regional theater and produces plays as well.

As for Myra—an unexpected benefit that comes with writing memoir is recollecting forgotten kindnesses. One of these occurred on my fourteenth birthday and involved Myra. Mom had insisted on giving me a party. I had not asked for a party. I did not *want* a party. But somehow my mother felt it her duty to give me one, although beyond buying refreshments, she did not appear concerned about the details. I invited a dozen girls in my class and dreaded the afternoon they would come over. What were we going to *do*? Yes, we'd eat piazza and I'd open presents, but what about before then? At fourteen, we were too old for birthday games. How was I going to fill the time?

My mother always said the things you worry about most never happen. She was wrong this time. On the day of my party, ten or eleven fourteen-year-old girls sat around my living room making self-conscious chit chat, waiting for the party to begin. I'd convinced myself it would just *happen*, that I'd casually suggest a word game or something dumb like Twister and things would take off from there. They didn't. I was in a panic as I strolled nonchalantly out of the room. "I'll be right back," I called over my shoulder, as if they couldn't wait for my return. Once in the kitchen, I wanted to fall on my knees in thanks when I saw that Myra had come home and let herself in from the side door. "You've got to help me," I hissed in desperation. "I don't know what to do. I don't know how to start the party!"

Myra did. The sister who used to teach school to neighborhood kids soon had my friends laughing and shouting out answers to some cool guessing game. She saved my party. I'd completely forgotten this until I began to write about her. Myra still plays the piano, but instead of making me and Julie Baherling dance to the sheet music of "Mame" and "Exodus," she's now playing "Let Me Call You Sweetheart" for the residents of a local nursing home in Glen Ellyn.

Gale is in many ways the happy ending. Since my visit with her in 2004—my "halcyon days" visit—her health and her spirit have only improved. So has her art. She no longer paints flat fields of calla lilies and blank-faced angels. Her water colors are rich and intricate, full of vivid color and emotion. Her most recent painting was of Circe surrounded by pigs who resembled various men from her past. "It's such a catharsis! I'm facing my fear of being old and decrepit and getting revenge at the same time. And the pigs are really well drawn! I told Andy if he ever gives me a bad tarot reading again, I'd put *him* in the picture. Let's see if he's so quick to tell me a handsome suitor's not a comin' for me!"

With all that she's been through, she still makes me laugh as no other sister does. Gale's watercolors recently caught the attention of an Evanston art dealer who has shown them in his gallery and is interested in setting up more shows. She's thrilled about this. I am, too. Gale's the one sister who knows, as I do, what it's like to work at your art for years with little validation.

And then there is Claire, the sister I hated and loved the fiercest. I called Claire about a year ago after learning she'd fallen off her bike from what appeared to be a bad case of sun stroke. There I was, a woman of almost fifty, dialing my sister's number with shaking fingers and a thumping heart. It's how I have always felt the half dozen times I've mustered the courage to call her since moving from Chicago. Claire was pleasant when we talked that day, but allowed not one chink of her former closeness to me to warm the cool of her voice. Maybe that's how *she* felt *I* sounded. It has been that way with us over the years: one step forward, two steps back, each sister somehow missing the other's cue. I wonder if just thinking about me calls up the same fury and tenderness in Claire that I feel sometimes when thinking about her. That, and immense sadness.

Not long ago, I spent a weekend with Katherine and David and had the opportunity to read what Claire wrote in their guest book during a previous visit. A questionnaire designed by Proust is printed on each page of this book, along with blank lines for houseguests to fill in their answers. Claire's answers were more light-hearted, more *witty*, than I expected. Just who was this woman with the precise script and the elegant mind? Did she ever think about her younger sister anymore? I felt a pang of longing for the Claire I had once known so well. Then I read another of her answers:

Q.   Who are your favorite poets?
A.   *None. I do not like poetry.*

Not, *I don't know enough poets to answer the question.* Not even, *I never read poetry.* Instead, a very crisp, very definitive, *I do not like poetry.*

Yet a few weeks after that visit, I received a letter from Claire telling me how much she liked my essay about Dad. She must have read "My Dad, Finally" in the online journal that published it. She told me I brought Dad to life for her—high praise from the daughter who loved him so passionately she could not bear to admit his shortcomings.

So my writing, at least, has served as an olive branch towards family I have left. *Is that all? I gave up Chicago, a city I loved. I gave up a dependable job. And now that I am fifty-one years old, what have I got? Publications in journals nobody reads. Two worthless Master degrees. This after twelve years of apprenticeship and my heart breaking again and again over rejection, over never being good enough.* It is easy to think this way when I wake in the middle of the night and doubts set in. This is the underbelly of the cheerful little bio I included in my introduction: "I have a good man who loves me, some dear friends, two cats I adore—and my writing." All true, but so is the fact that Marc and I fight over credit card bills, and we live from paycheck to paycheck, and I sometimes wonder if my writing is any good at all, if even one poem will survive me.

But it couldn't have been any different. Despite the doubts, despite the heartache, I have no regrets about making writing—not children or career or money, but writing—my priority. It wasn't, for me, as if I had a choice.

I like to think my mother knew I would return to writing poetry one day. I was, after all, the daughter she never worried about. She told me that more than once, the woman whose voice I still hear in my mind. I will not pass on my mother's genes, but I have done what I can to pass on something else: the childhood she gave me. The home where she raised me and my five sisters. The husband and sisters she loved. I kept the promise I made to myself and to her that dull winter morning when my mother told me she wanted to write down her stories.

That satisfies me deeply. Sometimes I feel without any irony at all what my mother declared to me in the last note I have from her: *our days of spring are arriving.*

The Tolf Family, circa 1960. From left, top row: My mother, Katherine, Lenore, Gale. Bottom row: Myra and my father holding Claire and Francine.